D0849177

# Nonprofit Investment
# and Development Solutions

# Nonprofit Investment and Development Solutions

## A Guide to Strategies and Solutions for Thriving in Today's Economy

**ROGER MATLOFF**

**JOY HUNTER CHAILLOU**

WILEY

John Wiley & Sons, Inc.

For general information on our other products and services or for technical support,
please contact our Customer Care Department within the United States at (800) 762-2974,
outside the United States at (317) 572-3993 or fax (317) 572-4002.

Wiley publishes in a variety of print and electronic formats and by print-on-demand. Some
material included with standard print versions of this book may not be included in
e-books or in print-on-demand. If this book refers to media such as a CD or DVD that is
not included in the version you purchased, you may download this material at http://
booksupport.wiley.com. For more information about Wiley products, visit www.wiley.com.

*Library of Congress Cataloging-in-Publication Data:*
Matloff, Roger, 1959-
  Nonprofit investment and development solutions: a guide to strategies and solutions for
thriving in today's economy / Roger Matloff and Joy Hunter Chaillou.
    p. cm. — (Wiley nonprofit authority series)
  Includes index.
  ISBN 978-1-118-30477-8 (cloth); ISBN 978-1-118-33416-4 (ebk);
  ISBN 978-1-118-33527-7 (ebk); ISBN 978-1-118-33197-2 (ebk)
  1. Nonprofit organizations—United States—Finance—Management. 2. Investments—
United States. I. Chaillou, Joy Hunter, 1969- II. Title. III. Title: Nonprofit investment
and development.
  HG4027.65.M338 2013
  332.67'253—dc23
                                                              2012038550

Printed in the United States of America.

10 9 8 7 6 5 4 3 2 1

# Contents

# Preface: Here We Are

What our economy has recently experienced is more than just a crisis. The wake of the Great Recession has left a paradigm shift for nonprofit leadership and their Boards as Fiduciaries. This shift has changed how Boards evaluate and document investment decisions, the risks they are willing to take, and the way these details are communicated to donors. There has been a significant transference in donor behaviors and motivations and consequently the emergence of an increased need for precise development strategy and measurement techniques for communicating impact. Nonprofit competition for philanthropic dollars is fierce, and all organizations—big and small—need to conform to new standards of accountability and transparency. This book has been designed to be read by anyone who is involved with a nonprofit at the leadership level. We attempt to provide a balanced perspective around the priorities of investment and development strategy, and bridge the gap between those with backgrounds in investment management, nonprofit management, administration, and fundraising. Whether the reader's role is that of volunteer or staff leadership, he or she will be able to learn something new from taking the time to read this guide.

We will introduce investment and development strategies, tools, and techniques in hopes of providing some keys to success in this post-Great Recession environment, and provide answers to the following questions:

- What are the lessons we can learn from this crisis, to protect nonprofits from unnecessary investment risks and funding shifts in the future?
- What steps can be taken by nonprofit leadership and advisors to ensure that Boards and investment committees are prepared to make prudent decisions to protect the organization's financial resources and ultimately its mission and impact?
- What steps should be taken now to secure financial stability in order to ensure sustainability so that the good work and critical missions can have impact now and perpetuate for future generations?
- What steps should nonprofits be taking in order to ensure a donor will continue to support their cause? How are donors making their philanthropic decisions? What information are they seeking? What tools are they using and to whom are they turning for advice?

## Background: Where We Have Been

Our country recently has been through devastating economic experiences, the effects of which have been and continue to be felt around the world. Essentially, the reverberation of decisions made across the biggest firms in the financial industry—taking on immeasurable amounts of risk—resulted in the obliteration of well-known multi-billion dollar investment companies and created a world of uncertainty for corporations, individuals, governments, and nonprofit organizations across the globe.

The walls of Wall Street came tumbling down in 2008. Lehman Brothers, Bear Stearns, and Washington Mutual filed for bankruptcy and fell off the map; others, like AIG, were crippled. The government concerns about bank stability encouraged mergers between powerhouse companies like Wachovia and Wells Fargo, and Merrill Lynch and Bank of America. Countless other investment companies experienced dramatic upheavals, limiting the extension of credit to other businesses. Who would have believed that in one year, both Chrysler and General Motors, symbols of preeminent American industrial strength and prestige, would both file for reorganization under bankruptcy laws?

So severe was the financial crisis, so close were the capital markets to unraveling, that the United States government took unprecedented steps as enforcer to the financial industry, to end the crisis and minimize the collateral damage. The Department of the Treasury was involved in shepherding the process of J.P. Morgan purchasing the remaining assets of Bear Stearns. The Federal government took further drastic action by investing in large national banks, insurance companies, and the auto industry, with those leaders navigating through the crisis, speaking *sotto voce,* that these corporations were "too big to fail." The Federal Reserve Bank, Department of the Treasury, and, at their urging, Congress, took dramatic action in the form of a stimulus package, to inoculate the economy from plunging into another Great Depression.

However, despite the stimulus legislation, which mandated the infusion of $787 billion, the aftershocks of the crises have been devastating and felt by all. Hundreds if not thousands of businesses shut their doors; individuals invested in the stock market saw no gain after a decade of investment; retirement savings vanished; and unemployment has been at an all-time high.

## Multiple Factors

Some may have clear recollections of the relentless daily news featuring countless market declines. As the Dow Jones Industrial Average plunged below 7,000, even stalwart believers in the equity market were taking a reality check—how far down could the markets go? As it happened, the year 2008 was the most volatile year in the securities markets since 1929. Two of the best *and* two of the worst days on record occurred in 2008; on October 13 and 28, the market gained 11.6 percent and 10.8 percent, respectively. And we witnessed September 29 and October 15, with the market sustaining stunning losses of 8.8 percent and 9.0 percent, respectively.

Looking back you may recall living through the media discussions in late 2008, recounting how the origins of the financial collapse had been seeded years before, when federal and banking policies shifted, loosening residential credit, allowing those Americans who had high credit risk to purchase homes. The easing of regulations during the Clinton era was well intended, to enable middle to low-income earners finally to enjoy the pride of home ownership. Their mortgages were bundled with others in complex financial packages and securitized as collateral debt obligations (CDOs). The purchasers of those packages fully believed that the mortgages underlying the securities would be paid to the underlying lenders and that the value of those CDOs would appreciate over time. It is when the CDOs on their books became devalued that the situation became worse.

As borrowers were unable to pay their mortgages *en masse* the value of the CDOs dropped, those insurance companies holding the financial portfolios that carried the insured value of the CDOs were called upon to pony up. But, what they had not expected was the cascading of failed CDOs, putting pressure on their balance sheets. Much of what occurred has been evocatively told in such books as *House of Cards* by William Cohan (Anchor, 2010; describes the collapse of Bear Stearns) and Andrew Ross Sorkin's book, *Too Big to Fail: How Wall Street and Washington Fought to Save the Financial System—And Themselves* (Penugin Books, 2010; the story of the decline of Lehman Brothers) that have focused on tracking, on an almost daily basis, the unfolding of events that led to the Great Recession.

What is most striking is the trail of destruction this crisis left in its wake. For all of 2008, the S&P 500, a standard measure of the strength of the U.S. stock market, declined by 38.5 percent (37.0 percent including dividends). From the market's apex to its lowest point, the market declined more than 51 percent (October 9, 2008 to November 20, 2008). Oil peaked in July of 2008 at $147 per barrel only to plummet to $35 per barrel near the end of December 2008, a sign that business and consumer demand had all but dried up.

During this crisis, the market declined more than 51.9 percent. Only three times since 1939, including this latest crisis, has the market declined by more than 40 percent. While a recovery during each recession took time, perhaps years, the average market increase after the two worst recessions was 84.2 percent. This leads us to believe that we will experience positive growth in our future.

As if the declining markets weren't enough to cause fear and suffering, simultaneously a number of Ponzi schemes were exposed beginning with investment manager Bernard Madoff pleading guilty to defrauding more than 1,000 individuals, families, and charities of $60 billion dollars. The Madoff scheme was coined the largest in American history. Families were devastated, some victims committed suicide, and some nonprofits shut their doors, while others shed staff and programs. Nonprofit organizations across the country had major donors whose wealth disappeared instantly and endowments were depleted as a result of Madoff's fraudulent activity. Subsequent to the Madoff scheme, many more Ponzi schemes were exposed when their culprits were unable to continue to fuel their confidence games with new money.

To complicate matters further, as unemployment rose in response to the economic downfall, so did the demand for social services. Homeless shelters, food banks, and social service agencies had to increase their services and enhance their programs. The need in communities around the country rose at a rapid pace as the resources funding those organizations declined or even dried up completely. Individual donors, feeling their own personal economic crises, began to reduce or stop their funding. Government agencies revisited budgets, and funding allocations changed or were cut entirely. With resources retracting and individuals feeling less wealthy, donors began to evaluate their choices and be more selective in their charitable planning strategies. High net worth individuals became more strategic in their charitable plans. Decisions about which organizations to continue supporting were made with great care and guidance from outside advisors—accountants, attorneys, and financial advisors. More than 67.5 percent of high net worth households consulted their accountant when making a charitable giving decision, 40.8 percent consulted their attorney and 38.8 percent their financial/wealth advisor.[1] Additionally, the list of charities was slashed in some cases from 10 or 12 to 2 or 3. Therefore, as the financial needs of nonprofits rose and the need for services increased, the dollars available retracted and the allocation of those dollars, and the selectivity with which donors were making donations was building as well. Enter the growing accountability and transparency standards. In 2008, the government unveiled the new Form 990 (*Return of Organizations Exempt from Income Tax*), fiduciary responsibilities of board members were emphasized and many smaller nonprofits were eliminated based on their inability to comply with the new reporting standards. The tone had officially changed as the business

---

[1] The 2010 Study of High Net Worth Philanthropy, sponsored by Bank of America Merrill Lynch.

of running a nonprofit efficiently and effectively became more relevant both for obtaining funding and complying with regulatory requirements.

There is no question that the challenging economic and investment climate and scarce funding resources have left us all, individuals, for-profit corporations, governments, and nonprofits alike, with a new reality. Specifically for the nonprofits, there is more competition than ever before, and boards and nonprofit leadership are forced to reexamine themselves as leaders, stewards, and fiduciaries. Leadership must have a keen awareness around risk, sound policies, and practices to make prudent decisions to preserve the mission and impact goals of the organization. Our theory is that sound policies and prudent practices, from investment consultant selection to donor communication and collaborative Board and staff practices, are essential in coping with consistent volatility, heightened need for governance and oversight, and generally growing expectations around accountability and transparency. Focusing on these issues will provide leadership with an opportunity for self-examination and empower them with tools to be effective stewards of donors' dollars and help them to attain and maintain a fit and healthy existence along with the kind of focus for-profit companies are compelled to have by the nature of competition in the marketplace.

For discussions in this book relating to nonprofit investments, we assume that the board of the nonprofit delegates these responsibilities to an investment committee. We recognize that in some nonprofits, the board acts as the investment committee, although we see an increasing trend for nonprofits to use a separate investment committee, given both the level of work and time required to manage nonprofit assets and the increased regulation of endowment management

## This Book's Setup

This book is intended to provide insight and easily adoptable principals for sound investment and development practices. Some of the topics are more technical than others. We have attempted to provide clear and basic definitions and examples throughout to facilitate comprehension of the more technical applications.

There is certainly more to managing a nonprofit's investment and development strategies than can be laid out in a couple hundred pages. However, by the end of this guided journey, regardless of a readers experience level in either strategy, he or she will have a strong basic understanding of the relationship between the two and the necessity for prudent practice around both. We hope you enjoy taking these lessons as much as we enjoyed learning them ourselves through practice over the years and putting our experience to paper through this process.

Each chapter is organized by key themes based on the broad chapter topic. The end of chapter questions are designed to help readers come up with one or two actionable ideas by leading them through the process of thinking about where their nonprofit stands relative to the strategies, solutions, and techniques. The questions are meant as a guide for readers to discover which issues are most relevant to their organization and help them begin to formulate ideas based on the suggestions in the material. Readers may discover that their organization has many challenges to overcome. It is important not to get discouraged by this, as identifying the issues and challenges is the first step to finding solutions and realizing the opportunities that will ultimately lead to success. Let us get started by reviewing history and its effects on the evolution of philanthropy and charitable giving.

Roger Matloff
Joy Hunter Chaillou

# Acknowledgments

To my family and friends who I consider the greatest *gift* of my life. Thank you for your support, love, and encouragement. You each provide me with unique inspiration for which I am deeply grateful.

*Joy*

To Erica, the *foundation* of my life, who has taught me that giving is important, but caring is essential . . .

To my children, Adam and Breanne, who have *endowed* me with much pride and joy . . .

*Roger*

# CHAPTER 1

# Philanthropy History and Statistics

The fragile state of our economy has had a severe effect on nonprofit organizations and how they operate. However, it has also provided us the opportunity to witness and reaffirm the deep philanthropic values of individuals in our country. Understanding a bit about the history and recognizing how our philanthropic culture is evolving will be very useful information as we begin to dive into the strategies and solutions for success in today's economy.

Individuals continue to be the single most important source of philanthropic contributions. Individual giving accounts for 88 percent of the total estimated U.S. charitable giving of $298.42 billion in donations made in 2011.[1] Additionally, donors are keenly aware of the increased needs that have arisen as a result of our depressed economic state. There has been an increase in giving specifically in the areas of human services, health organizations, and public-society benefit organizations. Loyal high net worth individuals have displayed an understanding of the immediate need organizations have to increase programs and services in our current environment. Statistics show them pulling back on growth project support like capital campaigns and long-term investments and increasing support for general operating expenses.[2]

What are the roots of this deep philanthropic nature and how has it brought us to where we are today?

## American Philanthropy

American generosity can attribute much of its origins to our Judeo-Christian religious tradition, influential philanthropists, our government, and taxes.

---

[1] Giving USA Foundation, Giving USA Report 2012.
[2] The 2010 Study of High Net Worth Philanthropy sponsored by Bank of America Merrill Lynch.

The first American settlers were compelled by the inclination to unite and satisfy local needs, such as the building of churches and schools. *Barn raisings*, in which the local farmers gathered to join together to help in building the essential structures for new couples, were routine. This experience, plus the fact that so many early settlements were religious in nature, set the precedent for our tradition of charity and individual efforts to promote the common good.

The French economist Alexis de Tocqueville wrote in his 1835 book *Democracy in America*, "In no country in the world do the citizens make such exertions for the common weal." Andrew Carnegie, who acquired an enormous fortune as a result of his work in the steel industry, was by 1901 devoting himself totally to philanthropy, which he said was the responsibility of every wealthy individual. He took seriously his famous saying, "The man who dies rich, dies disgraced." By the time of his death, Carnegie had given away 90 percent of his fortune. He, John D. Rockefeller, and others established America's first private, grant-giving philanthropies.

In 1914, Frederick H. Goff established the Cleveland Foundation, our nation's first community foundation; it was quickly followed by many others. Just 16 years later, 21 cities had community foundations with assets exceeding $100,000. Today, there are more than 600 community foundations possessing assets in excess of $25 billion and in total, more than 76,000 grant-making foundations that give away over $45 billion annually!

In addition to the examples these incredible philanthropists were setting, the country was experiencing the advent of the personal income tax. It began in 1913 and was followed by the decision four years later that individuals could take a tax deduction for charitable giving. This event in our history created a tremendous spur to charitable contributions. As millions of Americans found themselves subject to the income tax for the first time during World War II, and given the patriotic spirit of the era, from 1939 to 1945, charitable contributions increased fivefold. Since then, charitable giving has continued to increase. During World War I, Americans gave the Red Cross more than $400 million, an enormous sum in pre-inflation dollars.

Additionally, during the Great Depression, the national government assumed a role in philanthropy that it has never entirely relinquished, though its focus has altered decade to decade. Funding was given to antipoverty and civil rights efforts, job training programs, and other social programs.

Now we have come to a point in our history where donors recognize the power of philanthropy. They are exhibiting confidence and dependence on the nonprofit sector as the primary provider for solutions to persistent needs and are focused on supporting broad-based non-governmental solutions. In a recent study more than 94.5 percent of high net worth households stated that they are more confident in the ability of nonprofit organizations over the state or federal government to solve domestic or global problems.[3] So, let's take a look at what these strong philanthropic values have translated into statistically for nonprofit organizations.

## Examining the Statistics

The development and evolution of American philanthropy is the envy of the world, and deservedly so. Many foreign countries are currently struggling to build a culture of philanthropy as they too feel the effects of economic crises and uncertainty and experience a retraction of government support.

According to Independent Sector (www.independentsector.org), in America 1.2 million charities and nonprofits support more than half of all hospitals, 58 percent of social service providers, 46 percent of all colleges and universities, 87 percent of libraries, and 86 percent of museums and public gardens. According to the National Center for Charitable Statistics, as of

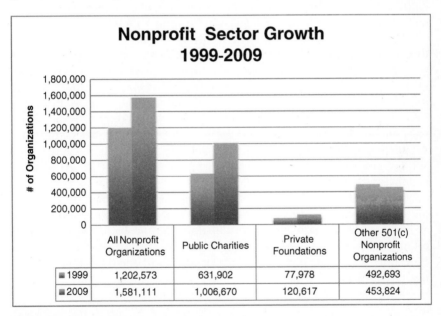

| | All Nonprofit Organizations | Public Charities | Private Foundations | Other 501(c) Nonprofit Organizations |
|---|---|---|---|---|
| 1999 | 1,202,573 | 631,902 | 77,978 | 492,693 |
| 2009 | 1,581,111 | 1,006,670 | 120,617 | 453,824 |

**EXHIBIT 1.1** Nonprofit Sector Growth
Source: IRS Business Master File 01/2010 (with modifications by the National Center for Charitable Statistics at the Urban Institute to exclude foreign and governmental).

---

[3] The 2010 Study of High Net Worth Philanthropy sponsored by Bank of America Merrill Lynch.

January 2010 there were 1,581,111 tax-exempt organizations registered with the IRS, up from 1,202,573 in 1999. This number includes public charities, private foundations, associations, chambers of commerce, and fraternal organizations. The number of public charities over this 10-year time period rose by 59.3 percent, making up 63.7 percent of all tax-exempt organizations. Private foundations increased by 54.7 percent, making up 7.6 percent of the total.

As recently as 2007, before the current recession, public charities reported more than $1.4 trillion in total revenues, nearly $1.3 trillion in total expenses, and nearly $2.6 trillion in total assets.

The depth of the economic crisis required nonprofits to increase their provision of services and assistance. Demand has increased for health and social services, counseling, and scholarships for schools. A 2008 Giving USA survey showed that the need for social services was up about 54 percent. The need for services continued to increase and caught some nonprofits in a bind, since giving was down. The same Giving USA survey indicated that more than 60 percent of social service organizations were taking steps to cut costs by cutting staff and reducing costs and services, due to funding shortages.

So, what happened to charitable giving during this time? According to Giving USA 2009, the giving climate could have been worse. Although people kept giving, they did seem to be more selective on where they gave. Overall, giving exceeded $307.6 billion, but giving was down by 2 percent from levels experienced in 2007. This was the first decline recorded by Giving USA since 1987, when we experienced a stock market crash and major systemic shock to our markets and the economy; individual giving dropped 2.7 percent, or 6.3 percent adjusted for inflation. Corporate giving dropped 4.5 percent or 8 percent in inflation-adjusted dollars. The 2010 study conducted by Giving USA revealed overall giving rose by 2.1 percent on an inflation-adjusted basis. Individuals, companies, and philanthropic institutions made gifts and pledges totaling an estimated $290.89 billion in 2010, an increase of 2.1 percent on an inflation-adjusted basis over a revised estimate of $284.85 billion the year before. As stated in the 2012 Giving USA Study, total giving from 2009 through 2011 increased by an estimated 7.1 percent. Individual giving rose by an estimated 8.5 percent, and charitable bequests rose an estimated 12.2 percent after seeing a decrease of 5.8 percent in 2010. The 2010 increase was the first since 2007, when the recession started, leading to the biggest decline in giving in more than 40 years.

Even as we move through this challenging economy, our culture of philanthropy as a country continues to be strong and a priority. More than 98 percent of high net worth households gave to charity in 2009[4] and the 2012

---

[4] The 2010 Study of High Net Worth Philanthropy sponsored by Bank of America Merrill Lynch.

Giving USA Report reported that the total estimated charitable giving in the United States rose 4 percent, representing $298.42 billion in charitable gifts. However, our current economic state continues to have a severe effect on nonprofit organizations because inflation-adjusted giving from individuals is at an almost flat 0.8 percent growth rate.

## Summary

Our philanthropic culture remains strong with healthy support and confidence of individuals in the nonprofit sector. However, there is a limited number of dollars and the competition for these dollars is growing. Amidst the current economic climate, many nonprofit organizations began implementing initiatives to cut costs, jettisoning mediocre programs and focusing on what they do best. With more than one million charities in the United States, to survive has become a Darwinian exercise—one must be fit, which translates to maximizing efficiencies internally with streamlined operations and administration, assessing costs associated with fundraising and programmatic initiatives, creating transparency of expenses and policies, performing prudent practices around endowment management and spending—serving as prudent fiduciaries and stewards of donor contributions and, most importantly, effectively communicating vision, goals, and impact.

Next up, Chapter 2 addresses one of the first things for organizations to focus on when taking steps toward evolving and thriving in this competitive environment: the roles and responsibilities of the board as fiduciaries.

# CHAPTER 2

# Fiduciary Responsibility

Nonprofits have a fundamental obligation to conduct their affairs, financial and otherwise, in a responsible and transparent manner. It's not only sound practice; it is intrinsic to the long-term vitality and success of the organization. The new normal that has evolved after enduring this economic jolt has resulted in heightened visibility and acute awareness of the compliance and noncompliance of prudent fiduciary practices. Board members carry the front line responsibility as fiduciaries protecting and preserving the prudent practices of the organization. Accountability and transparency are the buzz words in our new reality and the board members are responsible not only for ensuring that the organization is in compliance, but making sure it is staying ahead of the curve in meeting the expectations of the IRS, the donors, and the community it is serving.

Nonprofit board members as fiduciaries should be focused on protecting the public interest: preserving donor intentions, fulfilling legal requirements, creating and maintaining legal documents such as bylaws and policies, maintaining the integrity of the organization by avoiding conflicts of interest, and ensuring effective leadership. As a fiduciary, board members have an obligation to the organization legally, strategically, and financially.

## What Is a Fiduciary?

In general, a fiduciary is anyone who acts for the benefit of another; in which the beneficiary relies on the fiduciary with trust and in which the fiduciary must behave with good faith, keeping uppermost in mind the best interests of the beneficiary.

An investment fiduciary is someone who manages property or assets for the benefit of another, or who exercises discretionary control of such assets, or a professional placed in a position of trust, providing comprehensive and continuing investment advice.

Traditionally, those considered to be fiduciaries include attorneys, accountants, executors, money managers, trustees of private trusts, certain investment consultants, and committee members for foundations, endowments, and retirement plans. Broken into its component parts, a fiduciary is any person who:

- Exercises discretionary control over management, or the management and disposition, of assets.
- Provides investment advice for a fee or other compensation, or has the authority to do so.
- Has discretionary authority over the organization's administration, whether it is exercised or not.

The duties imposed on a fiduciary are significant, with legal ramifications if not properly exercised. There is a common misconception that outsourcing administration or consultation to others means transferring the fiduciary responsibility. Fiduciary status always remains with the fiduciary and cannot be delegated away to another or a third party, though there is a reduced liability through the use of a qualified consultant or co-fiduciary. The fiduciary capacity is established not from a title, but through the actions and responsibilities imposed by the functions of the position.

The execution of fiduciary duty is also not in simply making good investment decisions or in selecting competent managers. Conversely, investment reversals due to major corrections in the market do not necessarily point to a violation of a board's fiduciary duty. It is required that the fiduciary have in place a proper process for making those decisions. In fact, the fiduciary responsibility can be said to be inherently based on process. It is anticipated that from a properly prepared and applied process comes untainted decision-making.

In fulfilling their duties, fiduciaries must possess a reasonable understanding of the available investment alternatives. In addition, proper and detailed records must be maintained which fully disclose the process and how the eventual decision was reached.

## What Are the Duties of the Fiduciary?

A fiduciary must strictly adhere to the mission of the nonprofit. This may seem obvious, but it is crucial to proper conduct. The primary obligation of a fiduciary is to protect the public interest and maintain the integrity of the organization. A significant responsibility falling under these umbrellas is managing the portfolio assets in the interests of the participants and beneficiaries. He or she is required to create, adopt, and follow the terms of the Investment Policy Statement, which is the formal statement of the nonprofit's investment strategy.

Simply put, since a fiduciary must exercise his or her decision-making in the best interest of the charity, faced with two investments of equal risk, he or she is obligated to select the one with the greater prospect of return.

The fiduciary must also act in the *sole* interest of the charity. No other considerations, no matter how important or praiseworthy, may affect it. If one board member is voting because they or their business will benefit from a decision, they have a conflict of interest. He or she must honestly provide full disclosure of all material facts that could in any way influence the decision-making process. They should not vote on a decision where they may personally benefit, so that their board actions are judged to be solely for the charity's benefit.

A fiduciary also has an obligation to perform his or her duties in a certain prescribed manner. A fiduciary must exercise the utmost care to acquire sufficient information to ensure the maximum protection of the assets. All these functions must be performed in good faith, truthfully, honestly, with integrity, and with moral principles and sound character.

Nonprofits are now such a significant force in our nation's economy, and investment vehicles have become so diverse and complex, that oversight is now more a demanding function of a board and investment committee. Today's board and investment committee members and managers face new and unprecedented concerns.

## Pressure on Fiduciaries from Increased Volatility

Nonprofits generally hold resources far greater than they have ever possessed in the past. The sums can be enormous and a bit overwhelming, especially to a traditional administration. Not surprisingly, properly and efficiently managing such a portfolio is often a challenge, and beyond the scope and experience of existing staff.

In the boom years of the 1990s, when much of this value was created, this was not a significant issue, since most responsible investments delivered a high rate of return, but with the meltdown of the stock market many nonprofits have found themselves in very difficult financial straits. Managing resources in such a problematic environment has proven beyond the abilities of large numbers of boards and managers, with adverse consequences for their organizations.

One of the lessons taken from the experiences of the last decade has been a heightened sense of risk aversion. The unprecedented growth in the value of assets in the 1990s, followed by an equally unprecedented drop in value and rate of return, has caused, in many cases, an unwillingness to engage in adequately aggressive investment out of fear of new losses and blame.

Though inflation has been at modern record lows during this time, given the overriding economic realities it cannot be expected to remain so docile indefinitely. Charities and nonprofits must be prepared for a resurgence of this asset-devouring specter. Funds too heavily invested in fixed-income vehicles can be potentially devastated by the resurgence of inflation. The targeted spending rate, 4 to 5 percent in most cases, can cut negatively into a portfolio in such circumstances.

Balancing future anticipated donations against future giving has never been more challenging. Being too conservative in approach can be as problematic as being too aggressive. The steady rise in investment income, along with a predictable donor pattern, adjusted to giving needs, is now a phenomenon of the past. Never before has the immediate future appeared so uncertain. Volatility in the market always exists no matter how an endowment seeks to avoid it. The recent level of volatility, not seen since the Great Depression, has shown how portfolios can be ravaged without balancing allocations among various assets.

## Protecting the Assets—The Prudent Investor

There is much harm the imprudent or dishonest fiduciary or investment consultant can cause or allow to happen. They can participate in speculative investments without proper research and information gathering. They can engage in excessive trading (known as *churning*) to produce transaction fees or engage in short-term trading of mutual funds to the same end. They can make unauthorized transactions or misuse funds, or even engage in fraud, forgery, or the misstatement or deletion of key information. For good reason, standards of conduct and expectations of behavior for the fiduciary have long been established.

Until the 1950s, the primary principle that governed the conduct of a fiduciary was called the "Prudent Man Rule." The phrase comes from an 1830 court decision in *Harvard v. Amory* in which Judge Samuel Putman addressed the issue that risk must be considered along with return, and wrote:

> *Do what you will, the capital is at hazard. All that can be required of a trustee to invest is that he shall conduct himself faithfully and exercise a sound discretion. He is to observe how men of prudence, discretion, and intelligence managed their own affairs, considering the probable income, as well as the probable safety of the capital to be invested.*

In practice, this came to mean that a fiduciary need only behave toward those funds entrusted to him or her in a prudent manner. Over the coming century, it was apparent that there were a number of holes in this approach when it came to application, because the Prudent Man Rule was a generalized standard that lacked a specific definition. In particular, it failed to address evolving potential conflicts of interest and the application of investments.

Then, in the 1950s, Dr. Harry Markowitz called into question a number of assumptions about sound investment policy for organizations. He eventually earned a Nobel Prize in economics for his work, and from it came the "Prudent Investor Rule." It has been summarized in this way: "Investments shall be made with judgment and care, under circumstances then prevailing, which persons of prudence, discretion, and intelligence exercise in the management of their own affairs, not for speculation, but for investment, considering the probable safety of their capital as well as the probable income to be derived."

The Prudent Investor Rule requires trustees to emphasize total return, not just preservation of capital. This had the effect of profoundly altering the responsibilities of fiduciaries and changed the nature of investments for nonprofits. Today, there are five steps in the recognized prudent process:

1. ***Analyze the Current Position.*** Carefully consider the mission of the organization, as well as the nature of the investment portfolio. These include brokerage relationships, accounting assumptions, legal issues, and formalized policies, to name a few. Thoroughly analyze the spending policy, using any of several accepted useful tools.
2. ***Create an Optimal Portfolio.*** Diversification is fundamental to managing risk. For this reason, asset allocation decisions are crucial. In any potential investment there are tradeoffs between return and risk. They are the key to sound investment. An optimized portfolio will have managed risk within a commonly accepted range and in compliance with a nonprofit's established Investment Policy Statement.
3. ***Formalize the Investment Policy.*** The investment policy of a nonprofit must not only follow the standards of the Prudent Investor, but it must be set down in writing. This serves as a guide to the fiduciary, ensures continuity in objectives, provides standards, and allows new trustees and managers to participate effectively in a shorter timeframe. It must include investment guidelines, allocation standards, and investment objectives, and set the standard for selecting investment managers.
4. ***Implementing the Written Policy.*** Understand that though trustees and managers will come from a variety of backgrounds and bring to a nonprofit a great deal of experience, they are held to the same level of expertise as a professional investment consultant. It is necessary that qualified professionals be included in turning the Investment Policy Statement into actual investments. Investment funds and managers must meet rigorous standards. Investment managers must also be a good fit for the goals of the fiduciaries.

5. **Regular Review.** Monitoring investment performance is as important as the other four steps. Performance should be regularly evaluated. The performance of investment managers should be compared to that of their peers and similar portfolios. Such regular review will allow fiduciaries to evaluate performance and will assist them in decision-making. It will also provide an opportunity for discussion by the board members and/or managers concerning possible changes or difficulties that might exist.

In the final analysis, fiduciary liability is not the result of the performance of the portfolio, but rather whether sound investment practices and processes have been adhered to.

As explored further in the upcoming chapter concerning investment policy statements, states have increasingly adopted the philosophy behind the Prudent Investor Rule and applied it to the investment of nonprofit institutional funds. Many states have enacted the UMIFA, the Uniform Management of Institutional Funds Act, and a law that adopted Markowitz's Total Return Theory (discussed in more detail in a later chapter.) But the latest version of the law, UPMIFA, the Uniform Prudent Management of Institutional Funds Act, adopts the measures of prudence articulated in the Prudent Investor Rule.

## Training and Education of Fiduciaries

Nonprofits are under a tremendous amount of scrutiny and practices of the boards are under a magnifying glass. The days are long gone where serving on a nonprofit board qualified as volunteer activity without the need for responsibility or accountability.

Over the course of the last several years, nonprofits have come under scrutiny for a variety of reasons. First, as happens with unusual regularity, certain nonprofits are exposed for unethical business activity. Just recently, the Chancellor and several board members of the University of Illinois stepped down after it was revealed that students with questionable academic records, children of prominent Illinois families, were being accepted over better qualified students, in violation of admission policies and standards. Other universities, including Princeton University and Tulane University, have been sued for using endowment funds for purposes contrary to initial donor agreements.

More universally, state attorneys general, who have standing to oversee the operation of nonprofit organizations in their states, have been much more aggressive in insuring that their citizens are protected from unscrupulous practices and that nonprofits in their states operate with prudence. Now more than ever the donors, prospects, the community, and the IRS hold board members accountable. They are expected to exercise their legal fiduciary responsibilities, duty of care, duty of loyalty, and duty of obedience in making sound decisions, protecting the mission of the organization, and serving as prudent stewards of the investments and spending practices.

Given the degree of their exposure, it is understandable that potential board members are now far more aggressive in scrutinizing organizations prior to engaging in a leadership role. They recognize they will be taking on responsibility for the nonprofit to be well-managed and they want to understand the extent of their personal fiduciary responsibility and exposure. Board members also understand the need for their nonprofit to withstand the spotlight of official and public disclosure should it ever be directed at them. They want to know and understand what their personal fiduciary responsibility is, if for no other reason than to protect themselves. The protection works both ways, having educated and informed fiduciaries ensures the nonprofit can stand up to the tests presented by the heightened awareness the public eye is having on the sector.

Training and educating a board member on his or her fiduciary role and responsibilities is essential to attracting new, qualified board members. Executive leadership provides new board members with essential training. They should provide guidance and tools to articulate the critical elements of sound fiduciary practices and responsibilities. Further, the next chapter discusses that the investment consultant should be able to play a role in guiding organizations through this educational process.

A typical agenda for the first period of training for a new board member would include:

- Description and discussion about the role of a fiduciary
  - Protect public interest
  - Fulfill legal requirements
  - Maintain legal documents, policies, and bylaws
  - Maintain integrity of the organization—avoid conflicts of interest
  - Ensure effective leadership
- Legal responsibilities and the meaning to each duty—care, loyalty, and obedience

The second period of training for new board members should include:

- Discussion about the strategic duties of a Nonprofit Board Member
  - Ensure that the organization's mission is being fulfilled
  - Define, reexamine, and redefine the organization's mission and purpose
  - Review the long- and short-term organizational strategic plan—set priorities
  - Approve policies and major financial commitments

- Ensure periodic evaluation of the performance of each program
  - Evaluating whether programs, services, and activities still help accomplish set goals
  - Asking questions—in this competitive environment, is the organization offering the highest quality most effective programs and services to meet our mission related goals?
  - Reviewing progress and methods used for measuring success and impact
- Review and discussion of the financial duties of a Nonprofit Board Member
  - Ensure the viability of the organization over time
  - Ensure adequate funding resources are available in order to sustain the organization and its programs
  - Oversee the financial operations through budget review
  - Draft and implement sound investment policies
  - Create policies that authorize and enforce accepted accounting procedures

The most able and qualified candidates have always been difficult to recruit. Providing for the legitimate concerns of those who function in a fiduciary capacity is a key step in favorably positioning the nonprofit for the years to come. Training and education assures prospective board members that the organization is committed to being compliant, and invested in cultivating successful, educated, and aware fiduciaries on their board. Having a formal training process will provide the fiduciaries with the support they need to perform their duties well, and enable them with the tools and resources to be actively engaged and effective community advocates. Additionally, this level of commitment to training and education during the new board member training process could act as another inducement for prospective board members considering joining the board.

## Increasing Government Regulation

Nonprofits have always been responsive to political forces, never more so than today. Ongoing scandals in certain philanthropies, as well as those on Wall Street, have only heightened regulatory interest. Through a series of regulatory and reporting changes, the government tightened its grip on the exempt organizations and accountability and transparency standards rose with each step. First, the Public Company Accounting Reform and Investor Protection Act (commonly called the Sarbanes-Oxley Act), passed on July 24, 2002. Although the document applied most significantly to public corporations, two of these policy and accounting requirements applied directly to nonprofit organizations. Nonprofits are now required to have a Whistleblower Protection Policy and a Document Retentions and Destruction policy, but it was from that point on that individual states created even more regulation and requirements for the nonprofit organizations. It is in the fiduciary responsibility of the board members to create, review, and revise these documents.

With the number of nonprofits growing exponentially, the diversity and complexity by which exempt businesses are being run, the IRS made the decision to revise the Form 990 (*Return of Organizations Exempt from Income Tax*) in August 2008. This was the first time since 1979 that the document had been significantly revised. The new IRS Form 990 was based on three guiding principles enhancing transparency, promoting tax compliance, and minimizing burden on the filing organization. The new 990 discloses information about key employees, calling out policy around executive compensation, listing board members, calling attention to the existence of policies including those related to gift acceptance, financials, programs, and governance practices making the document multi-purpose— not solely as a tax-related requirement, but as a primary piece with information for donors and the community at large. Very specifically the Form 990 asks an affirming question to the board members confirming their review and acknowledgment of the document and its contents. Although the new form created a more complex reporting requirement for nonprofits and increased board member responsibility, it also provides organizations with an opportunity to be strategic, show a high level of commitment to transparency, and hold themselves accountable to the high governance standards that are being set by the IRS, their donors, and their community.

Finally, over the last eight years the IRS designed and expanded its website to include myriad resources and information for nonprofits. Specifically, they added a document titled the *Life Cycle* covering, in detail, governance related, reporting, practices, processes, and procedures for organizations to be in compliance around accounting and governance related topics. It's highly recommended that new and current board members become familiar with the Life Cycle document, specifically the area covering Governing Board and Governance and Management Policies as a guide to building sound governance practices for the organization on which they are serving.

## Protecting the Mission

In addition to their legal- and investment-related responsibilities, the fiduciary has a strategic responsibility to protect the mission of the organization as indicated in the second period training outline. They are expected to make sound decisions and protect the mission of the organization in addition to serving as prudent stewards of the investments and spending practices. Their responsibilities are not limited to the business of the nonprofit, but the practices and preservation of the nonprofit and the impact it is having in reaching its mission goals. Additionally, they are the key connectors between the community at large and the organization.

Protecting the mission is a multifaceted responsibility. The key responsibility for the board in this area is first and foremost to ensure that the organization's activities, program, and spending are in alignment with the mission of the organization and that the activities and efforts are consistent with the mission. Most importantly, the board is responsible for not only ensuring alignment, but also revisiting the mission if it is not in alignment and redefining it if necessary. This is easier said than done in many instances. The process of reviewing what the core competency is of the organization and making necessary changes to the organization's mission is a strategic process and board members need to think outside the box or as perhaps on the edge of the box. Thinking on the edge of the box means that the board as a group must continuously practice the exercise of thinking strategically and creatively about the following:

- What does our organization stand for?
- What is our purpose?
- Who do you serve?
- How do you serve them?
- What is your impact goal?
- What is the impact that you are having currently?
- What is your vision—the impact you would like to have in the future?
- Are all of the above in alignment with your current mission and vision statements?

The answer to the last question may be no. And then what?

Board members engaged in regular discussions about the mission-related review questions listed here will stay ahead of the game and develop keen awareness around the core purpose and competency of the organization. They will recognize when it's time to change, shift, or adjust the hows or the whats of the organization's focus. The key and most important element to that practice and ultimately the awareness is to recognize when it's time to change or shift the focus of the organization in order to reach existing goals or when it may be time to change the goals in order to meet the mission-related objectives.

Preserving and protecting the mission is not always about "doing what you've always done." What if what "you've always done" is not getting the results you've always gotten? Many nonprofits continue to move in the same direction they always have because that is all that they know. It is typically when someone new is brought into the mix, a new board member, staff member, or volunteer, that the questions begin being asked and the organizational leadership may at that point become introspective and analytical about mission. Board members can get caught up in the business of the nonprofit—the policies are in place, the annual review of the Executive Director, identifying funding gaps—and all of these activities represent the fiduciary responsibility of the board members. However, it is important to keep balance and perspective around the importance of the strategic responsibilities of being a fiduciary and not focus solely on the business policy of the organization.

## Effective Use of Professional Consultants

It is no longer expected that a fiduciary necessarily possesses the wide range of specialized knowledge needed to make informed investment decisions. The investment world has simply become too complicated. But it is expected that in designating investment management specialists, due diligence will be exercised in the process. In the context of a nonprofit, the board—and any committee delegated by it to assist it in making investment decisions—still has an obligatory role in all investment decision-making. For this reason, the proper selection and supervision of professional consultants is vital.

Investment management consulting is still an emerging profession, so care must be exercised in making such a selection. Given the heightened level of scrutiny nonprofits now face, the potential adverse consequences for fiduciaries, and the often-complex nature of investing and maintaining a large portfolio, such experts have never been more valuable. They can unburden a board and managers from the persistent details that inevitably accompany investment decisions and direct them into sound investment vehicles. The next chapter discusses the attributes of a good nonprofit investment consultant and goes into detail about the selection process.

## Valuable Resources

The best known and most highly respected organization of professional investment consultants working with non-profits is the Investment Management Consultants Association (www.imca.org). It provides professional recognition, ongoing education, and information on the evolving industry, as well as services for its members. It is an invaluable resource for fiduciaries. Additionally, one of the only educational resources for nonprofit chief financial officers and investment committee board members to learn about cash management and investments is NACUBO (National Organization for College and University Business Officers). The website and annual conference are rich in information and valuable resources. (www.nacubo.org)

Other useful locations for information of all kinds relating to charities are Charity Navigator (www.charitynavigator.org) and GuideStar (www.guidestar.org). Founded in 2001, Charity Navigator has quickly established itself as a major source for information relating to American charities and should be regular viewing for any board member or manager. Charity Navigator has developed a star rating for charities in terms of their efficiency, transparency, and impact. The website provides metrics on how the organization evaluates nonprofit efficiency. Just like not all colleges agree with the methodology of *U.S. News & World Report* regarding how they calculate the best universities and colleges in America, not all charities are happy with Charity Navigator's rating system. Nevertheless, the ratings are available in the public domain and board members as fiduciaries should be aware of the how others, including prospective donors, would perceive their nonprofit through the prism of Charity Navigator's evaluative process.

GuideStar is a leading source of nonprofit information and provides information and resources for more than 1.8 million IRS-recognized nonprofit organizations. GuideStar is a trusted resource by donors, grantors, organizations, and professionals across the country. In addition to providing detailed reports about the organizations, they conduct an annual compensation report study, *GuideStar Nonprofit Compensation Report*; they also collaborate with other organizations such as the Nonprofit Finance Fund to bring products and services to the nonprofit community to educate organizations on ways to maximize the impact of their financial analysis. GuideStar has multi-level memberships and the baseline information can be accessed for free and is commonly used by donors as a reliable and respected reference tool for gathering information in the decision-making process when they are considering maximizing the value of their philanthropic dollars.

Finally, another key resource that charitable organizations and board members should be aware of is BoardSource (www.boardsource.org). BoardSource, established in 1988 as the National Center for Nonprofit Board by the Independent Sector and the Association of Governing Boards of Universities and Colleges, is an excellent education and training resource. They have a plethora of tools and resources created with their mission in mind, "BoardSource is dedicated to advancing the public good by building exceptional nonprofit boards and inspiring board service." They, like GuideStar have a number of articles and postings available without membership, but many of the resources are accessed through an annual membership subscription.

## End of Chapter Review Questions

Here are some questions to consider and answer after reading this chapter:

- What does it mean to be a fiduciary?
- What are the key areas for prudent fiduciary practice as a nonprofit board member?
- What are the procedures in place for creating investment and spending policies?
- What are the practices for providing continuous review direction and oversight?
- What is your process for mission preservation, review, and revision?
  - Do you regularly conduct a governance assessment and review by-laws and governing policies?
- Do you have a strategic planning process?
- Are you ensuring periodic evaluation of the performance of each program?
  - Are you evaluating whether programs, services, and activities still help accomplish set goals?
  - Are you asking questions—in this competitive environment, are you offering the highest quality most effective programs and services to meet our mission related goals?
- Are you reviewing progress and methods used for measuring success and impact?

## Summary

In this chapter we discussed the vital area of fiduciary responsibility; a term that is consistently growing in significance to nonprofit organizations. We discussed what it means to be a fiduciary and went over some key considerations in making sure that your fiduciary responsibilities are being properly met. We touched on the government regulations that govern those who act as fiduciaries as well as the basis for these regulations in the Prudent Man Rule.

Coming up in Chapter 3 we discuss the roles involved in running a nonprofit portfolio in this new era. We go over the different individuals and groups who make up the fiduciaries of an organization as well as detailing how to ensure that we are filling these roles, such as investment consultant and investment committee member, with individuals who will not only meet the basic needs of these roles but fit well into a nonprofit from all perspectives.

# CHAPTER 3

# New Roles for the "New Reality"

Today's environment is one of increased volatility, inherent risk, elevated accountability, and transparency standards. Volatility is a key risk factor. The greater the volatility the more the risk to the portfolio, and in turn, the more the risk of not meeting the mission goals of the organization.

Risk must be managed consistently. One of the most relevant and obvious effects of the last 10 years of economic uncertainty has been the radical market volatility. 2008 was the most volatile year since 1929. Two of the best and two of the worst days on record occurred in 2008. Interestingly, there were two days in October 2008 (13 and 28) during which the market gained 11.6 percent and 10.8 percent, respectively. But we had to live through September 29 and October 15, where the market sustained daily losses of 8.8 percent and 9.0 percent, respectively. During this crisis, peak to trough, the market declined more than 51.9 percent. Only three times since 1939, including this latest crisis, has the market declined by more than 40 percent. For all of 2008, the S&P 500 declined by 38.5 percent (37.0 percent including dividends). From the market's apex to its lowest point, it declined more than 51 percent (October 9, 2008 to November 20, 2008). Oil peaked in July of 2008 at $147 per barrel only to plummet to $35 per barrel near the end of December 2008, a sign that business and consumer demand had all but dried up. While a recovery during each recession took time, perhaps years, the average market increase after the two worst recessions was 84.2 percent. So, we had hope, however the rollercoaster ride had already taken its toll and had a dramatic effect on endowment portfolios.

There are few organizations that did not feel the repercussions of the extreme market volatility and declines over the last four years. The question has not been "did the endowment fluctuate in value?" The question has been "why?" What was the core cause of the decline in the endowment assets? Many organizations have spent an extraordinary amount of time reviewing their investment-management strategies to help them determine if the decline in their endowment was due solely to market forces, leadership, or advice. Did the investment committee act without a process? Did the hired professional investment advisors provide them with prudent advice based on their mission-related objectives of providing programs and services to the communities they serve, or was the focus on outperforming benchmarks?

## The Investment Consultant

The consequences of this economic crisis on nonprofits have made us think that perhaps the traditional role of the investment consultant needs to be revisited. It's not just about asset management any longer; a new paradigm of consultant is needed. Investment consultants structuring investment portfolios in this new, less-predictable market need to understand the overarching needs of their nonprofit clients. They should have a grasp of how money is raised, encourage and facilitate good governance practices, and whenever possible help improve the operational efficiency of the nonprofit by getting involved in guiding prudent practices around policy and procedure. These are the ideal attributes for an investment consultant managing endowments and nonprofit assets.

The individual or team must have:

- An understanding of behavioral investing (a term further described in future chapters)
- Possess knowledge and expertise around traditional layers of investment management consulting
- Provide assistance in the development of investment policy statements
- Provide an assessment of nonprofit risk tolerance
- Evaluate the degree of investment risk each investment committee member is willing to assume
- Suggest an asset allocation
- Conduct a manager search and selection
- Consistently deliver comprehensive performance evaluation

But within and beyond these important tasks are others where expertise is essential to effectively serving nonprofits in this environment, the New Normal. They must have:

- An understanding of who gives and why
- Proficiency in the factors affecting charity efficiency
- The ability to provide ongoing fiduciary training and endowment development consulting

This support and expertise is critical to the ultimate success of the nonprofit. Selecting the right consultants as part of the nonprofit leadership team has never been more important than right now. Prudent investment management process, investment selection, and governance practices are equally important and crucial for both the operation of the organization and the ability to attract and retain donors. The investment consultant should guide the investment committee through the steps of establishing, measuring, and maintaining prudent practices. The following lists provide an outline of some basic expectations organizations should have of their consultant:

## Monthly/Ongoing

- Provide timely industry updates of nonprofit prudent investment practices
- Interact with the executive leadership team to find out what's happening with the organization and their mission-related programs, events, and fundraising goals.
- Participate in major fundraising or mission related events/community activities
- Serve as a community advocate whenever appropriate and the opportunity arises

## Quarterly

- Conduct quarterly performance and investment policy statement compliance review
- Suggest investments and discuss opportunities
- Recommend rebalancing or asset class additions/subtractions

## Annually

- Provide an Investment Policy Statement review, update, and revisions
- Have a Spending Policy discussion in which you review, update and make revisions if appropriate
- Provide fiduciary training (as was described in the previous chapter)
- Provide assistance through the annual audit process

Having a consultant who is actively involved with the organization and a part of the process will foster the education and awareness necessary for investment committee, Board, and executive leadership to proactively maintain a level of knowledge and accountability around the endowment performance rather than scrambling with the market conditions as they come and being faced with underwater endowment situations and the need to backpedal and analyze the what or why of the situation as they did four years ago.

# The Investment Committee

The investment committee is made up of a subset of board members, typically investment professionals. These volunteers are typically respected in their community for their extensive understanding of and experience in the capital markets. Many of them are passionate about the mission of the organization. However, they are not necessarily experienced in the business of nonprofit cash management and investment needs or aware of how the strategic development plan initiatives are going to affect the endowment. This is where the role, advice, and expertise of the right investment consultant can be very effective and essentially mandatory in the orchestration of sound prudent institutional nonprofit investment-management practices. As alluded to earlier, the investment consultant should have both the experience and understanding of the markets and an equal understanding of the nonprofit sector and the effect of market fluctuation on the ability for the organization to meet their mission goals. As the key advisor to the investment committee, they will ideally lead the committee through a process of making prudent investment policy and tactical investment-related decisions keeping mission advancement a top-of-mind priority, reviewing key market and sector trends, and evaluating revenue resources.

# Fundraising and Finance

The right consultant will provide and encourage an integrated approach and organizational philosophy, which can equip staff, board members, and committee members with a better level of understanding of the implications and consequences of their actions. This integrated effort is very specialized, one very different and far more demanding than that of the traditional investment management consultant.

It's not only the investment consultant who needs to rise to the occasion and be a well-rounded resource to their nonprofit clients, the leadership volunteers and staff of the nonprofits must have a clear understanding of the markets and how the current economic climate could affect their efforts to reach goals, provide services, and fulfill their missions. Nonprofits will benefit greatly by a stronger collaboration between the investment and fundraising teams. There should be mutual and equal awareness of the development and the investment strategies, philosophy, and decision-making process alike. Organizations should insure that the fundraisers know the process by which money-management decisions are being made and the volunteer leadership responsible for investment management should have ample knowledge of the implications of their actions on fundraising strategies for current, capital, and endowment initiatives. As organizations strategically adjust, advance, and organize around the new normal reality, this synergy and communication between the volunteer leadership and staff will provide the nonprofit with a unique opportunity and strategic advantage around donor communication. Keeping in mind donor expectations around accountability and transparency of nonprofit operations and endowment management has escalated to new heights in this increasingly competitive environment.

## Selecting the Right Investment Consultant for Your Organization

In an environment where there are myriad investment professionals and numerous investment firms to work with, it is critical to select the right consultant as a partner. Not every investment consultant understands or has expertise in the area of nonprofit asset management. Those who have been managing nonprofits or sitting on investment committees for any length of time know that. However, it doesn't stop all or any consultants from trying, approaching organizations and asking for the business—so, how does an investment committee sift through the candidates and what should they be looking for?

The initial part of the selection process is to find an investment consultant with whom the committee is comfortable and one who effectively communicates ideas and concepts. Obviously, if the committee finds a personality to be annoying, cloying, or oppressive, the group will not establish and maintain the kind of essential relationship its obligations and common sense dictate.

Keep in mind that financial and investment concepts can be presented in an overly complex, jargon-filled manner that is off-putting and needlessly confusing. These concepts are not great mysteries and can be articulated in down-to-earth simple language and writing. For all the new financial vehicles and the myriad names given to them, basic sound investing principles are essentially unchanged.

An investment consultant can be affiliated with a large financial services company, one that is a household name, or they can be independent. The most important step in identifying an investment consultant is to determine their qualifications and experience. Certain professional designations such as Certified Investment Management Consultant (CIMC), Certified Investment Management Analyst (CIMA), or the equivalent, can be very helpful. The investment committee should know the number of years of specialized experience the consultant has. His or her areas of expertise should include:

- Modern investment theory
- Investment policy development
- Investment management

- Manager selection
- Performance monitoring

The greater the experience and knowledge your potential investment consultant has, the more likely it will be that he or she will perform ably.

Everyone wants to work with his or her friends, trusted colleagues, and networks. It is very common for new foundation executives, board members, and investment committee members to suggest and recommend their investment advisor be given an opportunity to manage the assets of the organization. There are myriad competent financial planners and investment professionals in our country. However, the key to selecting the right professional for nonprofit asset management is to have appropriate filters and criteria. It is essential, more now than ever, to have an investment committee with a written process and policy around investment consultant selection. Agreeing on a process and having a policy for selecting a financial consultant is crucial. In addition to asking for the prospective consultant's background, bio, and references, organizations should use these questions as a guide when searching for the right advisor:

- Do you have other nonprofit clients?
- How many endowments do you manage?
- What is the average assets under management (AUM) for those nonprofit endowments?
- What is unique about your management or consulting style and technique?
- What is your goal when managing assets for nonprofits?
- Do you have the ability to manage to Socially Responsible Investment criteria?
- What type of organizations do you work with? Is there one area of the sector with which you have more experience?
- How will you partner with us in our fiduciary responsibilities?
- What type of education and training will you provide in addition to your investment management services?
- What are the biggest issues you see causing challenges or opportunities to the nonprofit sector?
- What are the key trends in the sector that relate to your work with us?
- Do you serve on a board?
- Do you actively volunteer for a nonprofit?

The interview process and asking the questions listed here will help the investment committee evaluate the consultant's asset management experience and provide the committee with a sense of the individual's understanding of nonprofits and how they operate, if they have their finger on the pulse of what is going on in the sector—which market conditions and economic factors they think will have the greatest/least impact on you as an organization, on your endowment, and ability to attract new revenue from donors, corporations, foundations, and the government.

It is also important to receive meaningful referrals from other investors with whom the consultant has done business. Be certain to fully understand the nature of the relationship and to weed out relatives, personal friends, or friends of friends doing someone a favor in making a recommendation. Ideally, the investment committee should speak to members of similar organizations and with managers who have had a long association with the prospective investment consultant. Anyone seeking such a position with your organization should have no difficulty providing a list of satisfied customers.

Additionally, the investment committee members should keep in mind that the kind of investment consultant they are looking for does not sell products and is completely free of other potential conflicts of interest. And if a potential consultant aggressively, or even subtly, directs the committee to a certain money manager, mutual fund, or other specific product, look elsewhere and end the association.

Though it is not commonly listed as a qualification, the ideal investment consultant will care about what you do and be personally involved on a voluntary basis in charities and giving. His or her roots will be deep and heartfelt. Such a consultant will bring a dimension and commitment no amount of money can buy.

The investment consultant should be interested in integrating into an organization and understanding its culture, mission, and goals. This connection is beneficial in making the consultant a more integral partner, and it is necessary as this investment consultant or team of consultants plays a critical role in helping the organization meet their goals though prudent investment management and spending practices.

## The Players on the Team

The resources that board and senior staff have access to in order to make prudent and educated decisions are essential. It is not just the investment consultant: the accountant, attorney, and money managers should also have nonprofit experience in order to provide the leadership team with the education, tools, and resources to stay current on sector-specific happenings and relevant legal and financial updates. One example of why this is critical is the recent change in institutional fund management and endowment accounting and reporting for endowments with the release of the Uniform Prudent Management of Institutional Funds Act. The evolution of UMIFA to UPMIFA was not a result of the crises beginning in 2008; however the guidance and expanded accounting and reporting elements were extremely relevant during the crisis.

The National Conference of Commissioners on Uniform State Laws began modernizing the UMIFA (Uniform Management of Institutional Funds Act) and in 2006, they finalized and released UPMIFA, the Uniform *Prudent* Management of Institutional Funds Act. In 2008, the economic environment, as previously pointed out, created an increased need for service and decreased resources. With donations dwindling and endowment values falling, it was the perfect storm.

Some of the restrictions placed on endowments and the method of calculating the total return for spending and distribution were limiting to a fault because if an organization cannot meet their program demand and mission goals, what is the point of their existence. UPMIFA received a lot of attention at this point and states began rapidly adopting the new guidelines to protect their nonprofit communities. One by one, because of economic devastation, endowments were underwater and there was a need for an increased level of oversight and flexibility for investment committees to protect their ability to meet mission goals. With the increased flexibility that UPMIFA provided to investment committee members came an increased accountability and reporting standard. The reasoning for decisions around spending that differ from the set spending policy must be documented. The right professional team is going to make the investment committee aware of the heightened standard and guide them through a compliant process.

## Investment Policy Statement

The Investment Policy Statement (IPS) is an organization's map to reaching its goals. It is meant to keep the organization in compliance with prudent investment standards and helps mitigate potential investment liability. Additionally, it defines the general objectives, describes the asset quality, it sets the asset allocation parameters, delegates asset management responsibilities to a financial committee or professional managers, and sets spending policy.

The right financial consultant will guide the investment committee through the process of creating the right investment policy statement for the organization. The investment policy statement should include the following elements:

- Fund portfolio's purpose and background
- Investment objectives in terms of
  - Return requirements
  - Risk tolerance
  - Time horizon

- Liquidity needs
- Legal and regulatory issues
- Unique needs and circumstances
- Investment guidelines
- Asset allocation
- Spending policy
- Performance standards and communication
  - Monitoring guidelines
  - Specific duties of service providers
  - Frequency and structure of reports

(Note that the elements of the Investment Policy Statement are covered at length in Chapter 7.)

Many times nonprofit organizations are started with board members and advisors who are friends with the founder or executive leadership. It is typically not a question of expertise, but a level of commitment, support, and time that is critical at that time. However, as the organization evolves, so does the need for strong experienced professional advisor support—investment, legal and financial professionals with nonprofit expertise and a finger on the pulse of the sector.

## End of Chapter Review Questions

Here are some questions to consider and answer after reading this chapter:

- How does your investment consultant stack up to the ideal attributes outlined here?
- Do you think of your investment consultant as part of your team? Do they understand your mission and goals?
- Does your investment committee have a formal and complete process for selecting an investment consultant?
- What is your current consultant doing to ensure you are at the top of your game in all of your prudent practices?
- How is the investment committee's process and practice around investment consultant selection and investment philosophy communicated to the front-line development team members for their conversations with inquiring donors and prospects?

## Summary

In this chapter, we learned what makes an investment consultant or advisor so valuable to an organization. We also delved into what separates a good investment advisor from one who isn't, and how to find the right fit for an organization.

Coming up, we discuss one of the most interesting phenomena to come to the forefront of investing over the last several decades. This is the nature of human psychology and how it impacts investing (also known as Behavioral Finance). Not only do we discuss a number of behavioral finance pitfalls that can hinder a portfolio's ability to generate solid returns without taking on undue risk, but we also go into detail on the group dynamics of human psychology in investing. Understanding behavioral finance will play an important role in making the right decisions for your nonprofit.

# CHAPTER 4

# Behavioral Finance

We are all human, all of the time. It is the nature of most of us to enjoy the sensation of speed, yet on an open expanse of highway we hold to, or close to, the speed limit. We might do so for safety concerns, or because we believe in obeying the law, or because we don't want a ticket. Regardless of our reason, we elect to suppress an all-too-human tendency.

Another example of human nature and impulse is the effect spring fever has on us. For example, late on a spring or summer day, as we gaze out our office windows, our human tendency is to want to leave work, get outside, and breathe the fresh air. But, most of us don't. We weigh the risk of not completing the necessary tasks of the day, missing client meetings, potentially getting fired depending on our role. Therefore, despite our human nature to enjoy nature at its best, we resist, suppress the feelings, and control our behavior. So, too, should it be when it comes to investing.

Investment committees are made up of individuals and the behavioral bias of those individuals can affect the decision-making process of the committee. Understanding behavioral finance and group decision-making is essential for investment committee members and more importantly for the investment committee chair. The investment committee chair needs to understand not only each individual's behavioral bias, but they must also have a grasp of the group dynamics, the influencers, and the fiduciary risk associated with the group being persuaded by a dominating personality or group bias. In his article, *Behavioral Finance and Investment Committee Decision Making,* Arnold Wood points out that "a thorough understanding of the behavioral biases of individuals as they interact in a group, such as a committee, requires that the committee chair proactively neutralize both the behavioral and social obstacles that impede a committee's successful achievement of its goals."

Mr. Wood's article highlights scientific studies and provides examples of how individual behaviors around finance and decision-making can pose an incredible risk to the investment committee's ability to make prudent fiduciary decisions. Additionally, he points out how these same behavioral biases can steer committees off track into a stock-picking mode versus remaining focused on the priority responsibility of guiding the course and overseeing the investment-management strategy based on the plan, which should be clearly articulated and documented in the Investment Policy Statement.

The investment committee must adopt a policy and exercise a strategy that may be contrary to the impulses of its members. A common human characteristic, though it has its matching opposite, is to want to make the big score, to make money in ways most people do not, to carve out a distinct character for ourselves as individuals who do not follow the pack. Most of us succeed in overcoming this tendency and recognize that while a measure of risk taking is necessary when investing, so, too, is caution. We understand on an unemotional level that steady and true is the best course. And so it should be for the board members of charities and nonprofits. They should come to the investment decision-making process with an understanding that while some risk is desirable, it must be controlled and balanced against the wisest long-term course.

## The Psychology of Investing

*Why* an individual invests money *where* they do can tell them a great deal about his or her self. In fact, an honest assessment of our finances, something we rarely if ever undertake, could likely tell us everything we need to know about our character and what motivates us.

Even in those situations in which we successfully suppress our emotional and psychological response in making investment decisions, emotions remain an active component for nearly everyone. The reason for this is because money is psychologically charged. When making major financial decisions it is not unusual for people to experience depression, anxiety, hostility, and anger, or on the other side, resignation and apathy. Psychosomatic illnesses are not uncommon. Counselors will tell you that couples fight over money decisions as much as they do child discipline and sex. Financial experts report that money, or to be more specific, debt, is the leading cause of divorce.

The concept of money is actually far more complex than most realize. Ask almost anyone why a hundred dollar bill, which is after all just a piece of paper, has value and they could not explain it to you. Yet, having money in your pocket and in your bank account is a satisfying experience, just as scrimping your way through the day only to return home to an ocean of debt is a destructive one.

More often than not, it's not about having enough to eat, or clothes on our back—it's about money itself. And so it should come as no surprise that our behavior concerning money and investments has deeply rooted motivations, many of them concealed from our conscious thoughts, nor should it be surprising that when it comes to money we lie to ourselves—a lot.

## Behavioral Factors and Investing

Financial decision-making is to a degree the result of rational thought and knowledge, but it is also the consequence of values, emotions, and bias. Though their effects are not fully understood, the stock market is known often to reflect the buying and selling patterns of a mass market driven by individual psychological forces. In fact, a fair degree of market volatility is considered to be the consequence of people behaving a certain way just because that's what others are doing, or because they are following a fad. The spread of certain mass behavior toward the market, either buying or selling, has been compared to that of the spread of an epidemic.

Investors generally believe they act independently of emotional and psychological impulses. They consider themselves to be rational and objective when it comes to making investment decisions. They tell themselves, and others, that they analyze key factors, obtain pertinent information, and then make calculated decisions designed to optimize their investment income.

To a certain extent this is very often true. What they do not acknowledge, though, is the role human psychology—our essential personality—plays in making many of the choices that lead to the final decision. For example, many years ago the investor may have had an unpleasant encounter with a broker at one of the major investment banking institutions. Never mind that the firm offers superior resources and advice, the investor never accesses any of their information, shutting him or her off from valuable insight.

People often make investment decisions that are irrational. They might possess an abundance of information yet still make the wrong choice. In so doing, they miss important opportunities to increase their rate of return and as a result earn less than they might otherwise.

Loss aversion is one of the powerful reasons why individual investors fail to match the rate of return experienced by institutional investors. When the market dips, they sell to avoid a greater loss and in so doing deny themselves the possibility of the greater gains. The same factors, on a much grander scale, led to mispriced stocks and a distortion of the marketplace in general.

Because of this, there exists a new field of research that studies persistent short-term mispricing that leads to long-term adverse consequences. It is called Behavioral Finance and has resulted in great strides towards explaining irrational decision-making by analyzing the emotional, behavioral, and psychological components of the process.

It has been found that even small improvements in eliminating behavioral factors from decision-making can have a very positive impact on overall performance. Consider the trained and experienced market analyst. It has been demonstrated that such an analyst has only a slight advantage over the market itself. Often they are only correct just a bit more than half the time. But the difference that comes in performance from just that slight advantage is profound. Compounding the extra rate of return over decades produces a far greater rate of return.

Consider a sports analogy. The difference between a baseball batter with a .250 average is not so very much, statistically, from one with a .300 average. Yet the one player will have a short career in the major leagues while the other will have a long, and lucrative, career. And the difference between their performances is only 5 percent. Or consider the money in a traditional IRA or in a 401(k) that is tax deferred. Match such a fund to one subject to current income taxes and the difference is day from night.

Eliminating, or even reducing, the human behavioral element in investment decision-making will have a profound impact on the future rate of return. It is for this reason that the average institution usually has a much better rate of return on investments than the typical individual. The primary reason for this is that institutions have in place policies and procedures to remove the human element from investment decision-making. One of the reasons why the average 401(k) investor today is doing so much better than the individual investor did in years past is the advent and use of mutual funds. Mutual funds are institutions that follow an established investment policy to guide their portfolios.

## Psychology and Decision Making

The human mind is very complex. It performs an incredible range of functions, both conscious and unconscious. If we lose the use of a portion of our brain, especially when we are young, the remaining portion will tend to perform the lost functions. Rational thinking is only one part of what our brain does. It's an amazing, and poorly understood, aspect of the human condition.

Understandably then, financial decision-making is a very small part of our brain functionality. Psychology plays a role in all of our decisions, even the ones we believe to be most rational. Even experienced and usually objective investment consultants may find their observations about a certain investment vehicle being shaped by a previous loss rather than from a rational analysis of the company.

Each question in a sequence that leads to a decision is set up, that is, is influenced, by the question and answer just before it. What this means is that a minor alteration motivated by emotion or psychology at the *beginning* of a discussion can magnify itself all out of proportion to the original distortion until a false decision, or at least, a less optimal one, is reached.

Since a minor factor in a series of questions and answers can greatly distort the outcome, behavioral finance researchers addressed the same phenomenon to understand certain persistent market inefficiencies. It is common, for example, for securities to be priced in ways that do not indicate their actual value.

Researchers have developed the following list of influencing factors:

- Overconfidence
- Anchoring
- Frame dependence
- Loss aversion
- Hindsight biases

Let's take a look at each of them in turn and how they influence what should otherwise be a rational, unemotional decision-making process.

## Overconfidence

People tend to be overconfident when making judgments. When people are asked to make a choice then estimate their probability of being right, they tend to believe they are correct eight out of ten times. In fact, they tend to be right seven out of ten times. This may not seem to be much, but consider that small changes in decision-making compounded over a series of decisions have a tremendous impact on the final result. Steer a boat only one degree off the correct bearing for your destination and you will miss it if the voyage is of any significant duration.

It is our nature to give ourselves credit for more virtues than we possess. This human characteristic is so universal that the occasional individual we encounter who thinks less of themselves stands out from everyone else. It is more typical for us to give ourselves credit for more skill, ability, and knowledge than we actually have. This is manifest in us through overconfidence.

Overconfidence, in and of itself, is not a bad thing; in fact, it has its advantages. It allows us to quickly discern conditions around us. It helps us to readily identify patterns from the past and allows us to exploit opportunities. Because of overconfidence we can often act more quickly.

But overconfidence can easily become rashness, and from it stems many behavioral mistakes in our daily lives. There is the finest of distinctions that separate a mistaken hasty judgment from a correct quick decision. When it comes to investment decisions, overconfidence usually results in a failure to properly analyze information and often leads to poor risk assessment.

Even when we guess, we tend to exhibit greater confidence in our answer than is justified by the facts. For this reason, overconfidence is a prevalent risk in making investment decisions because a crucial aspect of the process consists of analyzing a finite volume of information to arrive at accurate forecasts.

## Anchoring

Before answering any question our mind instinctively seeks a reference point. This allows us to find a context for the question and from that context elicits our response. Behavioral finance analysts call a reference point an *anchor*, while the context is referred to as a *frame*. We rely very much on anchors and frames to identify and rationalize the information we take in at any given moment, even though neither of them may be based on established facts. Regardless, we use them to interpret information and make our predictions.

Say a traveler is in the American Southwest one summer, having been raised in Seattle, Washington. He hears thunder and looks to the sky. His frame of reference, that is, how and when rain occurs in general, and his anchor, how often it rains when the sky is cloudy and there has been thunder, allow him to make the immediate decision that it is about to rain, and rain for an extended period of time. He hurries indoors and is surprised to see everyone else going about business as usual. In fact, there isn't an umbrella to be seen. The error he has made is based on his experience, which is true and reliable for Seattle, but does not apply to the specific hot summer conditions of the Southwest where the air is very dry and cloud cover is not extensive or lasting. At most there will be a brief shower, though much of the water will evaporate into the dry desert air before it strikes ground. The sky will be clear within moments. What he expects will not happen.

Analysts would use another example. In mental anchoring we are guided in the specific by general principles we take from our life's experience or by extending events with logic. Consider a tossed coin. Toss it enough times and heads and tails would result exactly 50 percent of the time. This is the principle in general. But in the specific our Seattle visitor might watch a coin tossed, say 10 times, and see it land on heads eight times in a row. From that he logically, and erroneously, establishes a mental anchor and concludes the coin is more likely to land on heads the next time it is tossed.

Such conclusions are all too common. Las Vegas and Atlantic City have built enormous, ornate structures and reaped billions in profits depending on this kind of logic. Simply put, people tend to see trends where none exist. They commonly make probability assessments based on relatively small samples, disregarding the reality that long-term performance may not reveal itself over the short term.

Investment consultants are not immune to this human tendency when they predict the direction of individual investment vehicles or the market in general. The two common errors are a belief that a trend will continue, or that it is time for a trend to reverse itself. In either case the error is in perceiving a pattern, the trend, from a short-term phenomenon. The reality, which should be known to the consultant, is that short-term market movements are random and that no trend exists.

Expectations based on early performance often also establish our anchor. Say a company posts record profits and market share for three consecutive years. We logically conclude the same thing will happen in the fourth year. Instinctively relying on such an anchor, market analysts routinely misprice stocks.

A proper analysis might reveal excessive debt, market saturation for the product line, increased competition, or any one of a number of factors that point to a sharp downturn, but our anchor leads us to believe that past performance will continue, at least for one more year.

## Frame Dependence

While anchoring is the danger for investment committee members when they believe they are analyzing data, the frame of reference is the pitfall when a committee member makes a choice disguised as a prediction. The frame is the way an issue is put. It is a variation of the old saying, "He who frames the question dictates the answer." An example of this concept would be: If an individual comes from a volatile, unhappy family as a child, they will tend to expect the same when they have a family of their own. And what they expect becomes their reality.

Many stocks declined in the immediate aftermath of the recent recession. Great numbers of these stocks were heavily sold off despite good underlying values in the companies. Yet as these stocks recover, slowly and continually, investment consultants are slow to recommend acquiring them. Their frame of reference had been rattled and because of that they failed to adequately exploit an investment opportunity. The facts were there, but the context in which they saw those facts had been altered and that adversely affected their judgment.

In such a situation the investment consultant must maintain discipline to be positioned to exploit such opportunities. The lesson to take from frame dependence is to keep broad comparative frameworks in mind whenever analyzing potential investments. It is very, very easy to see only the little picture and lose perspective.

## Loss Aversion

For most people, losing hurts more than winning feels good. It's why most people don't gamble very often or risk very much when they do. This aversion to loss strongly influences investment decisions. Most people will not accept the chance for a 15 percent gain if there is a matching 15 percent chance to sustain a loss. Analysts have estimated that the fear of loss is twice as great as any pleasure from making a gain. What this means is there is a tendency among investors to avoid the possibilities of loss, even though such an approach greatly diminishes the prospects for significant gains. This aversion to loss is a powerful influencing factor in any investment decision-making process.

## Hindsight Biases

While these behavioral predispositions influence our decisions about future investments, they are also influencing factors when considering previous data. Just as modern historians churn over past events in light of today's perspective, so too do investors recast what has taken place in their past. Identified biases include:

1. *Recentness.* People tend to view the most recent events as being more significant and meaningful than those that previously occurred. This is especially the case if the recent event or events have been dramatic or surprising. The effect is to prevent us from putting them in the proper context of a long-term framework. This tendency distorts our consideration of previous performance, and that can cause current and future misjudgments.
2. *The House Money Effect.* Playing with house money has a liberating effect on most investors. In other words, if our investments have done well we tend to be more aggressive and risk-taking with the increase because it is not money we put into the pot. Gains are considered less tangible and less valuable than the money we earned from our work. This returns to the principle that we have a strong psychological response to money. All money, from whatever source, whether it is from our labor or our investments, is and should be of equal value in our mind—but it is not.
3. *Regret.* Regret is a powerful emotion, one that can dog us all our days. It is not uncommon to experience continuing regret for actions or misdeeds

that occurred 30 and 40 years ago. So powerful is regret, and the guilt that often accompanies it, that it can become the single greatest influencing factor in our life.

When it comes to investment decision-making, regret can cause even investment consultants to take away the wrong lesson and compound the error by making wrong future decisions. The allure of regret is that we can never know with certainty what a contrary action would have caused. We might very well regret that alternative just as much had it occurred, but since we didn't experience the result of the alternative action, no regret is attached to it.

For example, a man regrets he never asked a certain woman out. It would have changed his life. The reality may not have been the experience he fantasizes. She might have said, "No," or they might have had a terrible time together. But he'll never know. Instead, he fantasizes about the life that might have been if only he had asked her out.

Regret is multifaceted. We tend to experience greater regret over near misses than for opportunities that weren't even close. In the one case, we can visualize the outcome, as it was so tantalizingly close. In the other, it was never really a possibility. So we feel regret with the first, but not the second.

We also are inclined to experience greater regret from an action we took that turned out wrong as compared to doing nothing and missing an opportunity. As it applies to investing this means that buying a stock that subsequently falls in value causes greater regret than failing to buy a stock that substantially rises. A realized loss is of greater emotional impact than a lost opportunity.

Take an investor who considered buying Microsoft stock when it released Windows 95. The investor decided at the time that Microsoft had pretty well run its course, that greater competition was looming and that the potential for future gains was limited. Since then he or she's seen the stock continue to rise. Presented with an opportunity to invest in Microsoft today, or to recommend such an investment, the investor may very well be influenced by regret and pass, again.

When investment decision-making is driven by regret it creates a bias against certain actions, even if they are perfectly rational and sound. Such warped hindsight causes misjudgments, usually unconsciously, and those misjudgments can have a severely negative impact on future gains.

## The Psychology of Group Decisions

The way we behave as individuals often stands in stark contrast to our behavior in a group. The military, in particular, has long understood how to cause a disparate collection of individuals to behave as a group. There is little battlefield value to be had from close-order drill, but everyone in the military does it as part of their initial training. Moving as one body, marching in step, are time-honored ways to create a feeling of unity within a group. The uniform and standardized grooming requirements are intended to serve the same purpose.

In the military, group consciousness and behavior serve an important function. In tests of small groups it has been established that they usually have a good track record in making certain decisions. For example, when asked to estimate the number of beans in a jar, a group of 56 students chose 871 when the actual number was 850, a remarkable level of accuracy and better than 55 of the students estimating individually.

While group consciousness and thinking is important to the military in particular and certain other organizations as well, it is not always desirable. When someone is asked to serve on a nonprofit board, the assumption is that he or she will bring to the experience their training, experience, and individual thinking. The assumption is that a decision reached by the board will be the best possible because each member will draw on those strengths and bring them to the process. But quite often that is not the case.

For a group to make a more accurate decision three factors must be present:

- Those involved must be unaffected by others' decisions.
- The likelihood of being correct must be independent of the likelihood of everyone else being correct.
- Each participant must be unaffected by the fact that their own vote could be determinative.

If any of these are broken, the effectiveness of a group's decisions quickly declines. Groups are subject to anchors and frame dependence just as individuals are. The expectation is that members of a group will exchange ideas with each other, bringing something different to the process. The idea is to be certain everything is covered. Errors on the part of any individual are expected to be corrected by the majority. The reality is quite different.

Considering an issue has the tendency to reduce variation. If the group reaches a consensus, that variation is diminished. The effect can very easily be to amplify rather than correct the bias of individuals in the group. Groups show an inability to uncover obscure knowledge, even if highly relevant, while focusing instead on the knowledge that is readily available to all, even if irrelevant or off point. Groups are also susceptible to the *cascade* effect; that is, once a strong opinion is articulated it becomes unlikely that anyone will speak against it and what follows is a rush to a decision. An adverse result of the group decision-making process is that each member will be very strongly committed to the outcome, even in the face of subsequent facts to the contrary.

The most significant difficulty of any group, or board, is the risk of polarization and the resulting groupthink. (Note that the next chapter covers the theory of *groupthink* in detail.) However, in short, the board ends up adopting a more extreme position than most of them individually held at the start of the deliberative process. Group thinking consists of:

- Consideration of too-few alternatives
- Lack of critical assessment of individual ideas
- Highly selective information gathering
- Absence of a contingency plan
- Actual feelings and opinions are suppressed
- Bad decisions are rationalized
- The group creates the illusion of invulnerability

Three accepted solutions for reducing group biases are:

1. *Use secret ballots.* A secret ballot tends to reduce the likelihood of social pressure on a board.
2. *Appoint a devil's advocate.* Naming someone to take the contrary position can be helpful, but only if it is a position they actually support.
3. *Respect other board members.* Openly acknowledge the contributions certain members bring to the process. If someone is trained and experienced in a useful area, their expertise should be openly acknowledged. His or her opinion should be given consideration. This tends to overcome the tendency of most board members to believe they know best on any subject.

## Behavioral Finance and Investment Consulting

One of the peculiarities of the human condition is that even when we are aware of a failing or susceptibility in our personality, we are often still its victim. If we have a sweet tooth, and know it, we still eat candy. If we indulge our children, and know it, we often still indulge them. And so, too, is our behavior concerning finance and investment decisions. We can understand all of this, even believe we are unaffected by it, yet still fall prey to our predispositions.

The investment consultant can demonstrate ways for investment committee members to profit from aspects of this tendency. For example, knowing that securities can become mispriced over the short term, they can provide insight to help identify such securities and advise on their timely acquisition. While financial markets generally price investments rationally over the long run, identifying the investment opportunities in the short term is an important skill the investment consultant brings to the table.

Investment consultants have long recognized the influence of behavior on financial decisions, and the industry has set in place certain investment strategies in response to them. They serve as safeguards against the mistakes that can occur because of these behavioral influencing factors. They are:

1. *Encouraging clients to balance investments.* An established balanced strategy, and rebalancing strategy, is perhaps the easiest and most direct means for avoiding the inherent bias in investment decision making. The theory is that investors should not be too dependent on a single type of investing or invested heavily in just one type of assets.

2. *Build and maintain a diversified investment portfolio.* Invest with a wide range of styles and maintain that approach in every market condition. Some styles do better than others or suffer less of a loss in certain market conditions.

3. *Screen money managers' databases.* They are regular buyers of mispriced investment vehicles and have in place those vehicles they require to help identify them. Such investments often have a greater rate of return as the market sees their undervaluation and pushes the price up.

4. *Follow a defined investment strategy.* An Investment Policy Statement wisely adopted then faithfully adhered to will reduce your tendency to be drawn into short-term market situations. It can serve to remove, or at least minimize, human bias.

5. *Manage asset portfolios with a knowledgeable team.* This approach should allow the inclusion of a number of investment perspectives. Each member of the team serves in effect as a check on the others. The use of a team, with its varying approaches, leads to an informed, rational decision-making process that generally eliminates behavioral biases.

Working with the money managers, the investment consultant should help to keep the investment committee members focused on long-term models that produce greater gains and avoid short-term strategies and overconfidence that lead to participation in the current market buzz as well as loss aversion when the market is down.

The consultant should expose the money managers to the broad frameworks of investment analysis and, when appropriate, arrange for them to meet with a variety of experts. This serves to enlarge the existing decision-making framework, broaden overall investment knowledge, and help them avoid or suppress behavioral biases. Recognition of such behavioral biases and their identification is an ongoing part of the education scheme. The consultant should also assist in identifying those investment vehicles which are undervalued or mispriced through behavioral biases so the nonprofit or charity can benefit from their acquisition.

The investment consultant should also assist the investment committee in learning more about behavioral finance, and should take the time to educate the board and managers accordingly. This is a rapidly growing field, producing ever more sophisticated results, which can positively impact financial investment decision-making.

Investment committees and Boards should expect the following from the investment consultants in his or her role of protecting boards and investment committee members from being victims of behavioral influence and personal bias:

- Assist in establishing an investment strategy that employs a very broad frame.
- Advise the committee to diversify assets to take into account market fluctuations and trends.
- Advise the committee to invest according to the Investment Policy Statement to exploit certain short-term opportunities and to eliminate, as much as possible, biases from the decision-making process.
- Remind the board of the common influencing factors of overconfidence, distortions caused by mental anchors and frameworks, disproportionate aversion to losses, excessive sensitivity to most recent events and to dramatic or unexpected ones, and the profound effect of regret on the decision-making process.
- Remind and counsel against letting loss aversion adversely affect future earnings.

Finally, investment processes must be constantly reviewed. Our human nature has an insidious way of taking control of any device we have created to provide an impartial process and warp it to our psychological desires. The more deep-seated the psychological motivation, the more it is concealed from our conscious mind, the more certain we can be that it has affected the very creations we have set in place to thwart it. For this reason, and others, we must constantly reexamine the investment practices and procedures that we have established.

## End of Chapter Review Questions

Here are some questions to consider and answer after reading this chapter:

- How many times a year do you review your Investment Policy and Spending Policy?
- What is your decision-making process as a group?
- How does your personal emotion and behavior around money influence your opinions?
- What is the method you will adopt to reduce group bias?
- How do you document your decision-making discussions?
- What are the elements of decision-making that come into play when you are making decisions for the organization versus your personal decisions?

## Summary

The investment consultant recognizes that every approach to investing contains within it a degree of behavioral bias, and it is an important component of their work to engage in a discussion with the investment committee about how behavioral biases can impact their decision-making. If it were purely a numbers game, computers could do it. There is always a human element in making sound investment decisions. It will be helpful for the investment committee to reflect periodically on its decision-making process, to minimize its influence of behavioral biases, and to be sensitive to how these biases manifest themselves in making their investment decision.

The next chapter discusses risk, group dynamics, and *groupthink* at length as a recommended modeling tool is introduced. Investment consultants should be implementing this tool when working with nonprofit investment committees to eliminate some of the behavioral and psychological risk around creating Investment Policy Statements and asset allocation strategies.

CHAPTER 5

# Understanding Risk

U nderstanding risk, its subtleties, its influence, and its effect on what we do and what we wish to do is a crucial part of the investment process.

In finance, risk means the fluctuations in the value of an investment vehicle. This is typically called volatility, and ranges from very volatile to stable. There are different kinds of risk. The general rule as concerns investment risk is that higher risk means greater volatility and with greater volatility comes a greater potential for gain. With lower risk comes less volatility but also a diminished likelihood of gain. In other words, there is always a tradeoff between risk and your expected rate of return.

There are so many factors contributing to a nonprofit's risk tolerance, individual behavior and biases, investment committee psychology, and most relevant *groupthink*. Blind Risk Modeling techniques provide extra measures to ensure prudent decisions are made around the Investment Policy Statement parameters and asset allocation.

## The Individual and Risk

Risk is an inherent factor in life and whether we realize it or not, it exists in all facets of our existence. It is in understanding and accepting risk that we become risk conscious rather than risk fearing, and the difference is often the distinction between the truly successful and those who fail. An investor who fears risk will never be able to realize the returns of the one who *understands* risk.

In finance, risk is simply a statistic, which like all statistics, can be reduced to simple terms. It can then be compiled into large groupings that create statements of probability, which are more trustworthy than any instinct could ever be. It is the ability to ignore instinct and follow these probabilities that allows wise investors to make significant gains, while risking no more than those who gain in baby steps.

It is important that investors, especially nonprofit board members, be able to ignore their instinctual fear and follow sound investment advice based on fact rather than emotion.

## Biases

There are many biases to which people are inclined. We may or may not be aware of them, but in either case they exercise a degree of influence over our behavior. Some of the most influential biases that affect us in investment decision-making are:

*Availability.* When an event is easier to imagine or recall we generally consider it to be more likely to occur. An example of this is the national crime rate. It has been falling steadily for some years, yet coverage of crimes that occur on the other side of the country is now greatly increased with instant reporting on 24-hour cable news shows. In addition, local crime is a staple on the local evening news shows. The result is that most people consider themselves to be more at risk from crime than they really are.

*Familiarity.* What we most dread is the unknown. Almost any risk we know is less feared than one about which we have little knowledge. For example, investors generally see greater risk in international vehicles than the statistics support.

*Illusion of Control.* We tend to underestimate risk when we are in control. For example, we are at far greater risk driving our car to the airport than we are flying on a commercial flight, yet we *feel* safer in the car because we have the belief that we are in control.

*Mood.* When we feel good, we feel lucky; when we feel bad, we feel unlucky. This affects how we behave during our daily life and it often determines how we make investment decisions.

To one degree or another we are all influenced by our biases. We often allow them to form our opinion and influence our judgment before we even realize it's occurred. More profoundly, they motivate us to act most of all when we deny they exist. This is why understanding them is so important.

## Investment Committee Psychology

No investment committee member wants the nonprofit to lose money. Besides looking bad in others' eyes, there is always the risk of having to defend your actions against accusations of misconduct. So when an investment, or investment policy, goes south, or appears to, there is a tendency for investment committee members to want to bail out quickly. They are, in short, more loss-averse than they are willing to sustain a loss for the likelihood of a future gain. So it is during a difficult market when the influences of behavioral finance most aggressively assert themselves.

The inherent tendency is for investment committee members to overlay their personal risk bias when engaged in the management of a nonprofit asset portfolio. This occurs even when the investment committee has been properly educated and understands the predisposition to do so.

Just as every organization, whether a for-profit or nonprofit, has its own distinct DNA, that is, its own unique character and makeup, so too does every investment committee. As mentioned in the chapter on behavioral finance, the psychology of the investment committee is determined by the psychological influences affecting each individual investment committee member. There is a misguided tendency to consider an investment committee, functioning as an institutional entity, to not be driven by the natural impulses of each individual member.

An important role of the investment consultant is to bring the findings of behavioral finance to investment committee members. This ongoing education is vital. In short, investment committee members often must be prevented from derailing a sound investment plan through their own good intentions, misguided direction, or behavioral biases.

All of us are subject to these influences. We like to believe we are not, but that is simply not the case. We are all motivated by complex emotions, past life experiences, the advice of friends and colleagues, and by our own innate character. This is why it is important to set in place those processes that eliminate the human psychological and emotional biases from investment decision-making.

It has been our experience that even when behavioral finance is carefully explained, the majority of the investment committee members often don't get it. They hear the words, recognize the behavior in others, but consider themselves personally to be immune, or to have successfully suppressed such motivations. They nod their head and respond appropriately then, often only a few minutes later, when called to participate in a financial decision, take part in it motivated by over-confidence, or regret, or . . . any of the other factors. No matter how well we understand something intellectually, we are still motivated by our emotional makeup, and our ability to conceal that from ourselves is enormous.

## Risk and the Fiduciary

As has been pointed out in this book, the fiduciary has a legal and ethical responsibility to the financial success of a nonprofit through prudent practices. If unethical decisions, or decisions lacking sufficient information, are made and they have a negative impact on a nonprofit, those in a position of fiduciary responsibility could be held accountable. This is a major source of stress for any fiduciary. The result, very often, is to create an excess of caution when making investment decisions for a nonprofit.

Undue caution actually harms a nonprofit by not allowing it to perform to its full potential. Underperforming can be just as detrimental to a nonprofit as ignoring risk in some instances. The investment consultant will assist the investment committee in determining its acceptable level of risk. This accomplishes several things, one of which is to eliminate the risk of being overly cautious with the nonprofit's investments. To do this they will conduct a study to gather information about each investment committee member's individual risk tolerance. Then, through an in-depth process called Blind Risk Modeling, they will determine the ideal cumulative risk tolerances for the nonprofit.

## Group Dynamics and the Nonprofit

Group dynamics is the branch of social psychology that studies interaction in social groups. When people are part of a group they tend to be influenced by one another in adverse ways and the resulting decisions may not be optimal for the organization. There are many different types of group dynamics, which may influence the decision-making of the nonprofit boards. These include:

> *The Political Model.* This involves the various members of a decision-making body using his or her own viewpoint to create a situation advantageous for his or her own position. The flaw in this type of group dynamic is that not all participants are fully aware of their constituents' knowledge.

> *The Process Model.* This involves the investment committee making decisions based on precedent and established guidelines. The flaw here is that while a bureaucratic decision-making process may ease things for the decision-makers, in the end it may not be what is best for the nonprofit.

> *Group Dynamic Shifters.* These are circumstances which change, or shift, the attitudes or mindset of decision-makers when they are in a group. There are two:

>> The risky shifter occurs when people meet and are comforted by the task of being part of a group. They tend to disregard danger and are susceptible to taking more risks, because they know they won't suffer the consequences alone. Such behavior can have a detrimental impact on nonprofit decision-making.

The first-shift occurs during a stalemate in the decision-making process. When a group cannot agree on something, as soon as one individual in that group shifts his or her opinion it is often human nature for each member to join sides with that first-shifter in order to come to an agreement. Again, this may not be in the best interests of a nonprofit because the individual who makes the initial decision to shift may not be the one most qualified to do so.

## The Theory of Groupthink

Psychologist Irving Janis found that group dynamics could have a significantly negative impact on the way groups make decisions. In 1972, based on such group behavior, Janis created a new theory he termed *groupthink*. Janis identified the phenomenon as the kind of thought that people engage in when deeply involved in a cohesive group, when the members' desire for unanimity overrides their motivation to realistically assess alternative courses of action. Groupthink can also be defined as a phenomenon when people seek undivided concurrence in spite of opposing facts pointing to a different decision. According to Janis, groupthink most often occurs on committees or in large organizations.

When people meet as part of a group they often make bad decisions. Individual members of a nonprofit investment committee may attempt to modify their own opinion in such a way as to match it to the perceived group opinion, resulting in decisions which aren't really what anybody individually wanted, but that everyone thinks the others want.

Groupthink can have several symptoms to which any nonprofit investment committee is susceptible. The first of these is what is known as the illusion of invulnerability. This is the false belief that when people gather and make decisions as a group they find it harder to believe they could be wrong, because they assume all of their peers in the group are double-checking each other.

Another common symptom of groupthink is a "belief in the inherent morality of the group," which stems from the same source as the illusion of invulnerability. People feel that the group is greater than they are as individuals. As a consequence, they assume a stance that everyone is working together for the "greater good." Since that is the case, their group decisions are inherently moral.

Another symptom of groupthink is "collective rationalization." This occurs when the group justifies a decision merely because the other members of the group support it. For example, if one investment committee member believes something, then the others will rationalize to themselves that it must be true because so-and-so believes it as well.

Psychologists have also noticed that out-group stereotypes can develop as a negative result of groupthink. When these out-group stereotypes exist there tend to be prejudices among the different divisions within a group. This very often includes a lack of respect for the opinions of other group members on nonprofit investment committees among those who have a greater perceived measure of power than the rest.

A serious symptom of groupthink is the self-censorship that often exists when groups are cohesive. This includes people not making known their own ideas, no matter how good or correct they may be, because they want to be a part of the consensus of the group as a whole. This symptom directly correlates to direct pressure on dissenters. When someone speaks out in a groupthink environment they are often ostracized for their different opinions or beliefs. This stifles open discussion and can have an incredibly negative effect on a group's decision-making ability.

One of the most important advantages to making decisions in groups is that there are many viewpoints, which help to identify or eliminate any faults or flaws in potential decisions. But that advantage is abandoned in a group-think scenario, which can be dangerous to the outcome of decisions.

What many people often do in groupthink situations is assume that there is unanimity, when there may not be. This often leads to group members taking silence to be acceptance, which is not a prudent practice in group decision-making. Group members should question anything they think is wrong; it's why groups can be so useful.

The final symptom displayed by groups that suffer from groupthink is the self-appointing of mind-guards. Mind-guards are individuals who protect the most important decision-makers from any dissenting ideas or opinions. For example, in a nonprofit this could be someone with expert knowledge or administrative power that notices dissenters among the group and quells their worries before they give strong utterance to their concerns.

## Related Decision-Making Problems

Along with the common symptoms of groupthink there are seven specific decision-making problems that are created by their presence. Those seven decision-making problems are:

1. Incomplete survey of alternatives
2. Incomplete survey of objectives
3. Failure to examine risks of the preferred choice
4. Failure to re-appraise initially rejected alternatives
5. Poor information search
6. Selective bias in processing information at hand
7. Failure to work out contingency plans

## Groupthink and Negative Power

Modern psychologists find examples of decisions that have been negatively impacted by groupthink throughout history. In American history, to name a few, these include the Pearl Harbor bombing, the Bay of Pigs Invasion, the voyage of the Titanic, the Space Shuttle Columbia disaster, and the bankruptcy of Enron.

The most explicit example of groupthink in recent U.S. history is generally accepted to be the Space Shuttle Challenger disaster. The cause of the shuttle explosion just moments after launch, destroying millions and millions of dollars of research and preparation and, most importantly, ending the lives of seven brave astronauts, was a faulty O-ring seal. The weather was simply too cold for the rubber to properly seal the gaps and contain the explosive force of the rocket engine. The rings had never been tested in such cold conditions but because of groupthink the responsible decision-makers disregarded the concerns of the scientists and engineers involved in that specific part of the mission. The Challenger team exhibited all seven of the symptoms of groupthink in their flawed process, which eventually led to the tragic deaths of these American heroes.

Another example of groupthink is the example of the many nonprofit foundations and individuals who were duped by the Ponzi scheme of John G. Bennett Jr. of New Era Philanthropy in Philadelphia. The announced concept behind how this was to work was interest based. New Era Philanthropy claimed it would match the donations of organizations after a certain time period, during which New Era would collect the interest on the principal given to them by donors to cover the costs of running their organization.

Groupthink occurred on two levels in this instance. The first was from within. Members of boards were influenced by groupthink from amongst themselves, meaning that the board of that nonprofit was acting as the in-group. The second level included the greater nonprofit industry. This was caused because one board was taken in by the New Era scheme, and subsequently other nonprofits felt justified in doing the same thing. They were all given the illusion of invulnerability simply because they were part of a larger group. When a nonprofit's board saw that a dozen other nonprofits had trusted their money with New Era Philanthropy they assumed it must be a good idea, otherwise those boards wouldn't have chosen to involve themselves.

They were wrong. What followed was a vicious chain reaction, which ended on the cover of the *Wall Street Journal* for an entire week in the middle of May 1995. In all, 185 organizations were duped by Bennett's New Era Philanthropy scam. According to the *Wall Street Journal*, there were red flags raised all over the place. And no one could understand, or explain, how so many intelligent people, controlling so much money, could have been so easily fooled into ignoring these red flags. This is a prime example of how groupthink can have a detrimental impact on nonprofit decision-makers and their organizations.

## The Blind Risk Model

Now, while groupthink may not always have as dire an effect on nonprofits as was the case with New Era Philanthropy, groupthink is still a serious problem, one that all nonprofit board members must take into account.

Leading groupthink psychologists have determined that the best way to eliminate the groupthink problem is to use an outside consulting source with the right experience. This process may be tedious and time consuming, but it is vital to the overall success of an investment program.

An outside consultant can conduct a group risk modeling analysis. Group risk modeling is designed to eliminate the groupthink that might potentially occur on a nonprofit investment committee. It requires all members formulate their conclusions on risk, both on an individual and on a group level. Our belief is that this type of risk measurement and analysis should be done so that each committee member can retain anonymity in order to prevent the negative factors inherent in groupthink. We will refer to this concept of conducting the group risk modeling analysis as the blind risk modeling process. The investment committee members, regardless of the influence they may have, are all considered carefully in the group risk modeling process. There are many steps to the process and the reasons behind each are critical to its development. It takes into account many factors that are essential in determining a proper asset allocation and investment policy statement, while avoiding the problems that can potentially occur.

The weighting system is one of the most important factors necessary for creating a successful model. This serves several functions, but most importantly, it helps determine which investment committee members will tend to influence other members of the committee. This aids in dealing with many of the issues created by groupthink.

In order to weight the individual investment committee members, the investment consultant should conduct in-depth surveys and interviews. The consultant will essentially create a resume for all of the members of the investment committee. This will allow the investment consultant to determine who knows what and how each opinion should be weighted in making specific decisions. For example, if certain members of the investment committee have experience in investing in stocks (perhaps at one point in their lives they were analysts or stock brokers) then those members should have a slightly higher weighted opinion than others when dealing with investing in the stock market.

If the other members of the investment committee are aware of the experienced individual's knowledge of the subject matter of the decision at hand, they will also be more likely to blindly trust them. This is not good. Blindly trusting anyone in a strong cohesive group environment often leads to poor decision-making.

The investment consultant should be aware of these pitfalls and be able to make the investment committee aware of them as well. Also, as an outside source, he or she will be able to identify solutions that lead to optimal decision-making.

## Understanding Individuals—Gathering Information

Knowing each investment committee member is essential for an investment consultant to be successful in guiding the investment committee through the process of developing the Investment Policy Statement and making sound and prudent investment decisions for the nonprofit. There are three vital areas of focus, and the investment consultant should have a developed process or questionnaire for gathering information: personal risk tolerance, motivation for serving on the committee, and general personality type.

### Sample Questionnaire Discussion Points

- Personal risk tolerance.
  - How would he or she manage his or her own money?
  - How would he or she react to certain events that occur from time to time in the stock market?
  - In adverse times, would the investment committee member step up to the plate, act on strong convictions, or would he or she flee from the decisions previously made?
  - Would the member increase the portfolio's position or would he or she want to sell and take the loss?
- Motivation for serving: An investment consultant should understand the reasons *why* the member is serving on the investment committee, as this can greatly influence investment decision-making.
  - What are some of the psychological benefits he or she receives from this service?
  - How long does he or she intend to serve?
  - How does he or she view the organization? Is there a personal connection?
  - How does he or she view the other board members?

- General personality traits: The objective in this section of the questionnaire or discussion should be to determine the key decision-makers.
  - Which members possess the strongest personalities?
  - Who will have the most influential voice (leaders)?
  - Who will be the listeners (followers)?

The process of conducting individual interviews with the investment committee members and focusing the discussion around these three vital areas will enable the investment consultant to more accurately gauge the process that will take place when hard times come, as they always do. He or she will have a better sense of which way the investment committee will be inclined to move, and who is most likely to exercise the greatest control in arriving at that decision. The more information the investment consultant has about the nature and behavior of the investment committee members, the better able he or she will be to support the committee in working together as prudent fiduciaries.

After gathering this information through a risk-modeling questionnaire, the investment consultant will be able to extract an aggregate score. Once they have this number they can run two asset allocation models. One is a typical mean variance optimization model that every proficient financial institution provides. The second is a downside risk model; that is, how much can the board really handle when the market goes down? This is useful in many ways, but especially so in selecting managers who are appropriate to the investment goals of a nonprofit and who will not derail the investment model.

## Assessing the Power on the Investment Committee

The process of conducting surveys and interviews will help the investment consultant to determine which investment committee members serve which functions for the nonprofit. There are essentially three types of power that tend to exist on nonprofit investment committees. These are:

1. *Expertise Power.* Those with expertise power are individuals who have experience in related fields. For our purposes, we deem those who have experience in the investment field committee members who hold *expertise power.*
2. *Contributory Power.* Those on the investment committee with contributory power consist of members who were given a position on a committee because of their experience in the nonprofit world as donors. These individuals have done their part as generous givers and in doing so have earned the right to sit on investment committees so that they may be able to help in the decision process. This is important if for no other reason than that their money, as well as that of other donors, is being

controlled by the decisions being made. They have the right to participate.

3. *Gavel Power.* This group most often consists of only the chairmen of the investment committee, though in very large organizations there may be several members who have gavel power. These are the investment committee members who sit at the heads of the tables, those who officiate at meetings, and those who may also be the public face of the nonprofit. Those with gavel power often have both expertise power and contributory power as well. This group is often weighted higher than the others.

The investment consultant will come to understand the decision-making process in great detail, and will also know how investment committee members interact with one another and know precisely how they fit into the structure of the nonprofit. Once identified, the next step in the process is to determine how these fit into the group risk model. Understand that the three groups mentioned here never self-identify. The investment consultant doesn't walk into a meeting and tell those with expertise power to raise their hands.

Once it has been determined what characteristics to attribute to each member on the investment committee, the weighting process can begin. The process consists of comparing all of the individuals on the committee and their various experiences and expertise. For example, those with gavel power are often weighted higher because they usually have the ability to sway decisions, while those with contributory power may be weighted lower.

The concept of the blind risk model is of great value here because someone with contributory power may be donating large sums of money to the nonprofit and therefore be unjustly influencing the decision-making of the investment committee. The weighting process properly determines how much of an influence this power should have, based on how well they can make a decision, rather than how they are viewed by other members of the committee or how much influence they believe they should have.

## Completing the Process

Once the weighting system is determined, then the group risk model is completed. The model consists of determining the individual risk tolerances of investment committee members in two scenarios. The first is their individual risk tolerances; the second is their risk tolerances as committee members.

The two are viewed together and through careful analysis are properly combined into what each individual committee member contributes to the risk tolerance of the overall investment committee. It is at this stage that the model becomes largely computer based. The values for each committee member are entered into a model created by a consortium of computer-modeling experts and financial advisers specializing in nonprofit investment management and consulting.

Along with those values are entered the requirements of the nonprofit, such as fundraising needs, legal limitations, grant, and gifting requirements—essentially everything that is at all related to finance for nonprofits. The model, through various mathematic functions, develops a precise and accurate risk tolerance for the nonprofit as an organization. This model is then linked directly to a program that determines proper asset allocation and specifies the investment vehicles that the nonprofit should be pursuing, based on their newly discovered optimal risk tolerance.

The group risk model is a crucial aspect of the investment process for nonprofits. Much time is needed to thoroughly complete it, but any time and effort, both on the side of the board and the investment consultant, is well worth it. There have been far too many nonprofits that have derailed a good investment plan out of fear of underperforming.

There always have been and always will be inconsistencies in the market; variables which cannot be predetermined should not change the way a nonprofit is invested. At times, small adjustments may need to be made, but the overall direction of the portfolio should stay the same for as long as the needs of the nonprofit remain unchanged.

The group risk model is the best way for a nonprofit to maintain an optimal course. The blind risk modeling process is a proven means for eliminating the problems of groupthink, for maintaining a steady course with investments, and for aiding in its growth.

## End of Chapter Review Questions

Here are some questions to consider and answer after reading this chapter:

- Do you feel your investment consultant understands the individual personalities and group dynamics of your investment committee?
- Do your committee members understand and know one another?
- Is there a healthy group dynamic on your investment committee? Are members working collaboratively to make decisions or is there one or two dominating personalities that may be compromising prudent group discussion?

## Summary

In this chapter, we discussed how risk relates to an organization and how understanding these risks takes a unique approach. There are a number of different dynamics when calculating risk for a group, as opposed to an individual, which need to be considered. In general, we learned that risks can be magnified when in a group; however, a group that is aware of these pitfalls can make advanced decisions to mitigate this risk and act like a true institutional investor.

In the next chapter, we apply the concept of risk to the science of portfolio construction as we delve into asset allocation and how the proper diversification and mix of assets can lead to a portfolio with risk return characteristics that go above and beyond what we traditionally think of.

# CHAPTER 6

# Asset Allocation

A sset allocation is the process for determining how to divide a portfolio among different asset classes. It is the initial step toward achieving a nonprofit's investment goals.

Theoreticians and practitioners agree that the asset allocation is typically the most important decision made by the investment committee as it is the most significant factor impacting the overall investment performance of a nonprofit's endowment. The reason for this is that asset allocation allows you to examine the correlation between the various risks and return levels and is the method through which risk is reduced. The asset allocation is dependent on the nonprofit's identified investment program objectives, tolerance for risk, and anticipated market behavior.

## Asset Allocation Analysis

While the actual asset allocation depends on the existing condition of the market, a portfolio's strategic asset allocation is the single most significant factor impacting overall performance. The greatest measure of return is the consequence of the asset classes selected and of the investment styles implemented and the allocation of each.

Not only does asset allocation produce the greatest portion of a portfolio's return, it is also the most significant aspect of the investment process under direct control of the investment committee. The various money managers will have discretionary control in selecting specific invest-ment vehicles, but it is the investment committee that designates the asset classes, investment styles, and asset allocation. It is also the investment committee picking the money managers with performance compatible with those decisions and the ability to implement the strategy in actual practice, setting in place the investment policy.

The investment consultant should guide the investment committee through the prudent practice of conducting an Asset Allocation Analysis, as a first step in setting the nonprofit's investment objectives. The Asset Allocation Analysis is intended to produce the proper mix of asset classes and investment styles to meet the investment committee's objectives. The analysis will focus on the desired rate of return and the established risk tolerance. It will seek to identify the level of risk the account is likely to incur in order to reach a given rate of return. If the investment committee desires to limit the nonprofit's risk exposure, the Asset Allocation Analysis will identify the gain that can be reasonably anticipated. Additionally, it will provide a broad range of asset allocation choices in addressing each of these issues.

As is the case in nearly all investment analysis, the guidance provided by the Asset Allocation Analysis is based on the assumptions and criteria selected which take into consideration the various categories of the nonprofit's overall investment program as well as the market's performance. The results can, and usually do, vary considerably from nonprofit to nonprofit, even those generally considered to be within the same peer group.

## Types of Risk in Asset Allocation

Risk and return go hand in hand. Risk, as it applies to life, is composed of exposure and uncertainty. Investment risk can include any number of factors. One of the leading concepts concerning investment risk is standard deviation, which is simply the measure of the dispersion of a set of data from its average. The more spread the data, the higher the deviation. In finance, standard deviation is applied to the annual rate of return of an investment to measure the investment's volatility.

There is a wide range of risks associated with nonprofit investing. Every investment vehicle faces different types of risks and to varying degrees. Risks for an investment can range from poor timing to the immediate need for liquidity. The investment committee has varying levels of control over the myriad risks and it is important for committees to understand each type and how it applies to the organization for which they are serving as a fiduciary.

The following are risk factors that can be controlled by the investment committee:

- Timing risk—Timing means when the investment is made.
- Tenure risk—The risk faced by holding an investment over a certain timeframe. This includes a shift in markets over time while holding an asset, subjecting the investor to inflation changes, even the risk of a company's stock becoming valueless over time.

The next group of risks involves those associated with owning stock in a particular company:

- Company financial risk—risk that a company will be excessively financed by debt. In such a case, a company is burdened with debt, which in turn means less growth and value.
- Management risk—risk that all companies face if they are poorly run. A company poorly managed will see drastic drops in stock prices, loss of dividend payments, and an inability to grow.
- Market risk—risk of the overall market not performing well, thus causing individual securities to suffer. The factors that affect market risk, among others, include liquidity, which is the risk that comes from losing value when selling an asset.
- Interest rate risk—risk that bonds will lose money when interest rates fluctuate, as they often do.
- Inflation risk—risk associated with the inflation of the money you place into an investment. It can be worth less when you take it out of that investment because of rising inflation during the timeframe in which you held the investment.
- Exchange rate risk—risk that the dollar might lose value in comparison to the currency of foreign countries; such a risk can severely harm investors with international assets.
- Reinvestment risk—risk that typically comes from investments that return principal over time. If at the time of assets being returned to the investor there are no investments offering similar risk/return characteristics an investor may be forced to reinvest their assets in a less than ideal investment.
- Industry risk—risk associated with the danger of a specific industry performing poorly.

The last common group of investment risk is *national* and *international risk*. These risks involve events and regulations that impact investment markets.

- National and international risk—risk that a country's economy will not perform well, which can cause many problems for an investor, including job loss, a downturn in stock prices, and many other factors which contribute to or are affected by national economy performance.

Investors also face two more very tricky types of national risk, which are *tax risks* and *political risks*.

- Tax risks—the risk that taxes will diminish your profit as an investor. The subtle downside of taxes is that a rise in taxes will frequently reduce the attractive nature of investing for many individuals, causing an overall drop in the markets.

■ Political risks—the danger of political changes such as prohibitive licensing or the election or placement of individuals into power who may be detrimental to an investment sector. These political risks can also include wars and trade embargoes.

The various types of risk which investors face arise on many levels. Investment vehicles will be differently affected by each of them, meaning that investors must deal with, or at least be aware of, all of them.

## Risk and Portfolio Performance

In the past, investors traditionally measured the risk of individual investments in order to maximize their returns. An investor would review a company, its past performance, its potential for growth, and other ratios and factors to determine the potential risk versus reward for a single stock. They would then invest in those stocks that best measured up. While this could result in safe returns, the results were often unpredictably disastrous.

With the knowledge that risk is *inherent* in investing, economists and finance professionals set out to minimize the negative effects of risk on portfolio performance. Dr. Harry Markowitz published his theory in a 1952 *Journal of Finance* article entitled "Portfolio Selection."

Markowitz's theory argued that the way to optimize the performance of a portfolio was not to analyze investments simply on a company-to-company basis. Rather, Markowitz suggested investors step back and look at risk of an entire portfolio. Markowitz determined that investors could counteract risk by shifting exposure (by allocating assets) and understanding that uncertainty cannot be changed. Markowitz's *Modern Portfolio Theory* plays to the natural unpredictability of the financial market by using the mathematics of diversification. Rather than picking stocks based on risk versus return, the model allocates and diversifies an entire portfolio based on overall tolerance of risk versus reward based on an individual investor, or organization's needs and goals. The opportunities and issues with Modern Portfolio Theory are covered in detail throughout the chapter covering Dynamic Portfolio Optimization. However for the sake of discussing best practices for developing a prudent asset allocation this chapter focuses on the concepts developed by Markowitz.

As part of his theories, Markowitz created what is known as the *Efficient Frontier*. This is represented as a curve along the graph comparing risk and expected return at varying percentages of asset allocation. It is along this curve that any portfolio should be located in order to maximize return at any given level of risk. *Modern Portfolio Theory* and the concept of the *Efficient Frontier* are Markowitz's contribution to the financial world. They are applied today in every prudent practice in determining asset allocation and they make it possible for nonprofit organizations to diversify investments in such a way as to optimize returns.

Markowitz understood that there is a very real, yet ephemeral, relationship between market volatility and return. In fact, risk is usually defined as a manifestation of market volatility, and in general, the greater the volatility, the greater the gain potential; the less the volatility, the lower the rate of return.

Even for the expert, defining risk can be elusive. Risk has many dimensions and must be analyzed from more than one perspective. These include the potentially adverse consequences of excessive market volatility, the maintenance of buying and spending power for the nonprofit, and the need to attain and sustain the rate of anticipated gain. This is all affected by the investment committee's risk tolerance, which, similar to what is seen with an individual's relationship to and behaviors around money, is a direct reflection of each member's tolerance level. Individual risk tolerance is a reflection of our life experiences and expectations for the future. In addition to the individual attitudes toward risk, there is a wide range of investment styles and a diverse selection of asset classes. Taking all of these factors into consideration, it becomes obvious what a vital role Asset Allocation Analysis plays as a tool for investment committees managing nonprofit assets.

In general, there are two approaches to risk tolerance:

1. *The basic asset allocation adjustment approach*—encompasses only the risk/return dimension of a stock, bond, and cash distribution. This is analyzed as:
   a. aggressive (a greater percentage of stocks)
   b. moderate (balanced percentages of stocks and bonds)
   c. conservative (a greater percentage placed in bonds)
2. *The style category adjustment approach*—relies primarily on the initial asset allocation and takes into consideration the timeframe and return expectations. From this the investment categories deemed to be most appropriate are selected. This approach tends to be more customized in implementing an investment strategy. Various levels of risk tolerance are combined with a wide variety of gain objectives and timeframes. There is a place for short and long-term expectations—conservative, moderate, and aggressive management styles. Maintaining the proper balance assures that the risk tolerance is adhered to.

# Preparing for Asset Allocation Analysis

There are three key factors in preparing for the Asset Allocation Analysis, including:

- Time horizon
- Desired rate of return
- Level of risk tolerance

While all three are important, the one that will have the greatest impact is the time horizon. The time horizon indicates how quickly the nonprofit wants to obtain a specific return on its investment. That specified return dictates the degree of risk to be assumed. From that comes the determination of the types of investments to be included in the portfolio. Most nonprofits are intended to function in perpetuity and it may seem at first glance that time horizon is of no consequence. But, the reality is that even a long-term investment program is subject to the adverse effects of short-term volatility.

The desired rate of return is the consequence itself of three interrelated functions:

1. Anticipated rate of inflation
2. The spending policy
3. Desired rate of growth

These three variables taken together comprise the total return objective. The greater the desired rate of return, the greater is the need for an extended time horizon and the acceptance of a more liberal risk tolerance. With these in mind, an asset allocation can be implemented with the capacity to generate the desired gain.

The Asset Allocation Analysis is a tool designed to assist the investment committee in making the most appropriate asset allocation for their needs. It is not a precise process that can unerringly predict the future and guarantee a given rate of return. However, if properly used the Asset Allocation Analysis can greatly reduce risk and increase returns.

## Establishing Risk Tolerance

Risk tolerance is a key component in devising the optimal investment strategy for a nonprofit and the single most significant issue of the Asset Allocation Analysis along with the timeframe, portfolio size, and return expectations. Risk tolerance is used to establish category allocations and to assist in determining specific investment vehicles. The essential prerequisite is to define all objectives and preferences in order to set in place the asset allocation strategy.

In considering any investment strategy or asset allocation the investment committee must also consider what is called *probability distribution.* This means taking into consideration every possible consequence and the related probabilities that could occur. The probability distribution can be continuous, as when all potential outcomes constitute a continuous sweep.

In determining risk tolerance there are at least four considerations:

1. Volatility is inherent in any investment so be honest in considering not just the potential gain, but also the potential loss.
2. Establish the organization's risk tolerance level before making any investment decision and assure that each investment conforms to it.
3. Diversify the portfolio into an optimal spread of investment categories.
4. Address risk tolerance and reestablish it no less than once a year. The market, even the nonprofit itself, will change, simply because change is inevitable.

Although risk is an important factor in preparing the Asset Allocation Analysis, it is elusive. To identify risk, it must generally be analyzed from several perspectives. These include the possible impact of a decline in purchasing power, the potential of creating greater volatility, and the need to achieve the anticipated gain. The Asset Allocation Analysis process will include a review of the various asset classes and different investment styles to assist the investment committee in determining which are appropriate and should be included in accordance with the nonprofit's established level of risk tolerance. Additional consideration should be made for the investment committee's actual experience in making investments.

## Establishing the Distribution Percentage

More from tradition than for any other reason, American nonprofits tend to follow a distribution of 60 percent stock, 30 percent bonds, and 10 percent cash or its equivalent. While it is true that statutes and regulations influence this mix, a much stronger motivator comes from the fact that most nonprofits follow this allocation. There is no financial or practical reason to consider such a distribution to be optimal. In Canada, for example, pension funds tend to have a mix of 40 percent stocks and 60 percent fixed income, while life insurance annuities are a strong component of European pension funds.

The reality is, each nonprofit is unique. Mission, investment objectives, portfolio size, and myriad other factors make a difference. This is but another reason why the Asset Allocation Analysis is such an essential step in guiding the investment committee in making specific investment decisions.

## The Market Analysis

What must also be analyzed to achieve an appropriate asset allocation is the market itself along with a determination of numerous other parameters. This part of the process begins by preparing a list of various asset classes and investment styles that the investment committee agrees to consider.

This is a four-step process:

1. *Allocation Parameters.* A well-balanced portfolio should not be skewed toward one style of investment or certain asset classes because of changes that occur from market conditions. To this end, it is important to establish the maximum and minimum allocation parameter for each class or style.

2. *Anticipated Rate of Return.* Within the Asset Allocation Analysis will be the projected return rates for each of the asset classes and investment styles. This is a challenge, as it is an attempt to predict the future. Markets traditionally have long periods with both above average and below average rates of return, and these deviations from the overall are seductively misleading. Therefore, the Asset Allocation Analysis will rely instead on long-term historical rates of return, coupled with economic forecasting, in arriving at a projected rate of return.

3. *Realistic Degree of Risk.* The Asset Allocation Analysis must not provide a false sense of security to the investment committee no matter how well-reasoned or how much information is included. The investment committee should review the analysis along with the actual degree of risk associated with each asset class and investment style. Drawing on long-term historical data, the analysis will include worst-case scenarios and realistic volatility levels. The investment committee should keep in mind that a track record of above-average performance in one class or style for a prolonged period does not mean that it will be repeated.

4. *Various Assumptions.* The time period selected can have everything to do with an historical average. For that reason, the Asset Allocation Analysis will include a number of time periods and will present a scenario for each of them using various probabilities for the anticipated rate of return and volatility. These will be used to put the assumptions to the test. The significance is that such an approach puts to rest any thought that the Asset Allocation Analysis is an exact science. It will show the importance of the assumptions and underlying data by producing very different outcomes in various scenarios.

## The Existing Portfolio

There are two options when applying the Asset Allocation Analysis to an existing portfolio. The investment committee can start with a clean slate or the analysis can be conducted to incorporate aspects of the existing investment portfolio.

The analysis is based on long-term historical performance of general investment vehicles and commonly accepted economic forecasts. Typically, the Asset Allocation Analysis would only reflect the performance of an existing money manager if the investment committee requires that stipulation. It is more common for the recommendations to come exclusively from the asset classes and investment styles themselves rather than the current money managers.

In cases when a specific money manager is identified for retention, the investment committee may also want to indicate the percentage of the portfolio assets to be allocated to that manager or managers. In any case, the Asset Allocation Analysis will make a recommendation suggesting an optimal deployment of the remaining assets consistent with the nonprofit's overall investment objectives.

## Rebalancing

Diversification not only applies to the investment vehicles within the portfolio, it is a technique many investment committees use with money managers. Several money managers with the same investment style can complement an asset class. This is relatively simple in the beginning, but once engaged, the actual performance, both of the asset classes and of the money managers, will begin to differ, often substantially, over time. The result can be that the careful balance of assets, investment styles, and risk goes askew. This is one of the important reasons for establishing parameters early on. Additionally, it is necessary for an investment committee to set a procedure and process in place for rebalancing the assets when necessary.

Such a process assures that regardless of the performance of any asset class or specific money manager, the portfolio will remain positioned consistent with the investment committee's established goals. When a formal rebalancing procedure does not exist, there is often a tendency to leave alone whichever asset class or money manager is performing well. When this occurs over time, the class or money manager can come to have an exaggerated presence in the investment program. Or there might be a tendency to simply rebalance the portfolio at random, without regard to overall or individual money manager performance, but based solely on the investment committee's perception of the state of the market. Neither of these approaches serves the long-term interest of the nonprofit's investment portfolio. The Asset Allocation Analysis will specify procedures to determine when rebalancing is required and how to go about it strategically. These procedures will include periodic examination of the market values of asset classes and the money managers. Additionally, maximum and minimum parameters, known as rebalancing points, will be established for each of the target allocations. The purpose of this process is to determine whether any of the rebalancing points have been reached. The rebalancing points and the frequency of reviews differ from nonprofit to nonprofit and must be set individually by the investment committee.

If the rebalancing point has been reached, it is an indicator that asset allocation is significantly different from the established target. At that point, the investment committee must consider whether or not to rebalance the portfolio. If rebalancing is undertaken, it is best to review all targets and asset allocations and make any necessary adjustments at the same time to bring the portfolio back within its targeted allocation.

If rebalancing is not done on a routine basis, it will have a significant, even a dramatic, impact on the position of the portfolio in the market. For that reason every investment committee should have a formal rebalancing process. This process will assure that the nonprofit is well served and that the portfolio reflects the optimal rate of return for the established level of risk.

## End of Chapter Review Questions

Here are some review questions you should consider and answer after reading this chapter:

- Do you currently conduct an Asset Allocation Analysis?
- How often does your committee review the asset allocation?
- Are you comfortable with the level of risk you have in the nonprofit's portfolio?
- Are you familiar with where your portfolio lies on the *Efficient Frontier*?
- Do you have a formal rebalancing process? Do you adhere to it?

## Summary

In this chapter, we reviewed some of the key concepts of asset allocation. We talked about the tradeoff between risk and return as well as what some of the major risks of investing are. We incorporated some elements on risk tolerance from the previous chapter into our understanding of asset allocation analysis and we also tied in how asset allocation can play a role in an organization's growth and spending.

In the next chapter, we apply this learning to the drafting of an Investment Policy Statement. These statements document determined asset allocation among a number of other topics and tie it all together in a codified demonstration of the understanding of fiduciary responsibility and nonprofit asset management.

# CHAPTER 7

# The Investment Policy Statement

The Investment Policy Statement (IPS) is the governing document for investment decisions. A properly drafted IPS will establish a framework for the evaluation and monitoring of the existing portfolio, set in place the guard rails for making all investment decisions, and assist in the retention or termination of money managers.

Specifically, the IPS should state the assumptions and expectations for the performance of the various money managers and outline the policies and procedures to guide investment decision-making and portfolio review. Additionally, it should address any administrative and other substantive issues relating to the investment program. Ideally, the IPS should be designed to make communication concerning the portfolio and asset allocation easier and more comprehensible for the investment committee. And, properly drafted, once adopted, it will greatly assist the investment committee in directing the investment strategy.

## The Elements of an Investment Policy Statement

A properly drafted Investment Policy Statement includes the following:

- Introduction: Explain the mission of the organization, the purpose of the policy, describe the assets it covers, and articulate the overall investment objective.
- Information about the Endowment: What does the endowment consist of? Are there only unrestricted funds, does it include donor restricted funds, donor advised funds, planned gifts, and so on?
- Responsibilities of the Investment Consultant
- Responsibilities of the Investment Managers
- Responsibilities of the Investment Committee
- Recognition of Current State Law: UMIFA or UPMIFA

- Discussion of Risk Tolerance and Time Horizon
- Asset Allocation Strategy and Spending Policy
- Performance Objectives, Standards, and Evaluation
- Investment Strategy
- Investment Guidelines
- Scope of Investment Transactions
- Meeting Expectations of Committee and Consultant

An investment committee without an Investment Policy Statement will find it difficult, perhaps even impossible, to determine:

- if the performance of the portfolio money managers is acceptable,
- whether or not the portfolio is positioned properly, or
- if it is on target to achieve the nonprofit's long-term financial goals.

Without an IPS, newly appointed investment committee members will struggle to know their roles, the role of your investment managers and Committee, and what the investment sentiment is among Committee members.

## Investment Policy Statement Functions

It is generally held that the IPS serves at least three important functions, including that it:

- *Assists* the investment committee, the nonprofit Board and staff, and the money managers in directing and pursuing the investment goals.
- *Provides* a window into the investment strategy and policy of the nonprofit to donors and prospects.
- *Assures* regulatory authorities and rating organizations that the nonprofit is conducting its investment affairs pursuant to a formal policy against which its performance can be effectively judged.

An IPS defines goals and objectives, outlines methods for achieving those goals, sets regulations and guidelines, specifies risk tolerance levels, prepares timeframes along which goals should be met, and prepares the investment committee for dealing with any changes along the way. A properly prepared Investment Policy Statement will set in place the necessary framework for the required evaluations the investment committee will need to conduct in order to make sound investment decisions.

Because nonprofits are unique organizations, every IPS must be individually tailored. The investment committee should work closely with their investment consultant to develop the optimal IPS for the nonprofit based on its unique needs and goals.

One of the most important aspects of the IPS is the actual investment policy, meaning the risk tolerances and asset allocation of the nonprofit. This portion of the IPS should contain a detailed summary of the conclusions reached through the Blind Risk Model and the Asset Allocation Analysis.

While a general statement concerning the nonprofit's investment objectives is helpful, what is also required is a narrative with sufficient detail to provide essential guidance in quantifying more specific objectives and the parameters or targets for those objectives.

A comprehensive IPS will include a discussion of the financial well-being of the portfolio in general, as well as the role of money managers and the issues concerning their performance specifically. The part of the IPS relating to the portfolio and its functioning will be prepared by the investment committee in collaboration with the investment consultant, and the specific issues concerning money managers will be developed through contact with them.

Achieving the nonprofit's investment objectives is essential, and so, too, is maintaining each investment committee and board member's fiduciary responsibility. It is not uncommon, when an investment program has failed to reach the desired objectives, that a donor or other party raises complaints. In the extreme situation where the state attorney general, representing the interests of the state's citizens, becomes involved, it is likely that an IPS and minutes of investment committee meetings will be of great help. This formal policy and documentation exhibit the investment committee's adherence to a formal process and attempt to follow the IPS.

A properly prepared IPS is of assistance in two ways:

1. Demonstrates that the investment committee has a process for addressing key issues
2. Shows that the board and investment committee have sought to fulfill their fiduciary responsibilities and are operating through an established process.

Resolving key issues when drafting the IPS is itself an important component of their fiduciary responsibility and of the portfolio management process.

## The IPS Provides Essential Discipline

As mentioned earlier, an Investment Policy Statement can protect a nonprofit from reacting emotionally to market gyrations. It does this by keeping investments on track regardless of the periodic blips on the radar which often cause needless concern. The well-drafted IPS serves as bedrock from which investment decisions will be made and in such times will minimize the tendency to react spontaneously to an adverse market condition.

An important function of the well-drafted IPS is that it is one of the best ways to eliminate the problems of groupthink psychology. It is also the best way to minimize the conflicts that may arise on any board.

## The Drafting Process

The actual process of researching, discussing, then adopting an Investment Policy Statement is extremely beneficial for the nonprofit. It compels that important long-term decisions be made, or if already made, the process will require reexamining those decisions. Decisions such as:

- Who will manage which aspects of the portfolio?
- What percentage of the assets will be placed into which types of investment vehicles?
- How much money does the nonprofit actually require to fulfill its mission?
- How much can it reasonably expect from donors?
- What should be the ratio of risk to gain?
- Who will administer the investment process within the nonprofit?
- How will the necessary information be provided to the investment committee and managers?
- What constitutes a conflict of interest?

These are just a few of the vital questions that need to be asked and decisions that have to be made. Most importantly, consensus by the investment committee must occur for each question before a single word of the IPS is drafted.

There is too much to be gained and too much potential risk for any of the required decisions to be rendered by an emotional response to the current market. Personalities will come in conflict, differing opinions will arise, and it is at such times that investment committee members will be sorely tested. But from the IPS drafting process can evolve a strongly united investment committee with a firm grasp of the financial issues the nonprofit faces. Additionally, during this drafting process, the roles of the committee members will clearly emerge. It will be obvious which members are leaders and who amongst the committee has the key skill sets to be making the specific investment decisions. This will naturally eliminate the inherent confusion that typically exists when financial decisions are made on an *ad hoc* basis, as they often are prior to the adoption of the IPS. The Investment Policy Statement will define and establish the nonprofit's Investment Policy to which the money managers will adhere. The day-to-day investment decisions should be within the province of those money managers, while policy and oversight belong with the investment committee and, ultimately, the Board.

The IPS is also a historical document that explains the nonprofit's mission, investment strategy, goals, purpose, process, and philosophy to those outside the nonprofit, such as major endowment donors, as well as to new board members. Once it is adopted and set in place, the IPS becomes a working document that is routinely consulted when new situations arise.

## Mission and History

The Investment Policy Statement may include a history of the nonprofit. This section will describe how and why the founders created the organization, defining its historical mission by stating what the nonprofit was intended to accomplish at the time of its inception. This is important, especially during the early stages of the adoption process. By formally stating the history of the nonprofit, investment committee members and consultants alike will become aware of, and dedicated to, preserving the intentions of the nonprofit's original donors and leaders.

Often going hand-in-hand with the statement of the history of the nonprofit, an IPS will state its mission since they are so closely related. This typically includes the current mission statement (potentially evolved from the original mission statement), the motivation behind that mission, and the financial means through which that mission can be accomplished. The mission statement helps to reaffirm the philanthropic approach of nonprofits, and allows boards and consultants to focus the investment objectives on a single outcome.

## UMIFA and UPMIFA

Often, an IPS will make reference to UMIFA (Uniform Management of Institutional Funds Act) or UPMIFA (Uniform Prudent Management of Institutional Funds Act). The National Conference of Commissioners of Uniform State Laws (NCCUSL) approved UMIFA in 1972 as a model statute for investment funds held by charitable organizations, governmental entities for charitable purposes, and endowments. A total of 47 states adopted UMIFA, excluding Alaska, Arizona, and Pennsylvania.

UMIFA opened the door to total return investing by adopting Modern Portfolio Theory. It broadened the ability for nonprofits to invest in a wide variety of asset classes in order to reduce overall risk. It also created a consistent body of law to guide nonprofit boards. It provided investment committees with direction to delegate investment management responsibilities as long as they managed within a general fiduciary standard of prudence and as offering instruction on the use of appreciated endowments.

In 2006, NCCUSL revised UMIFA to provide additional language on a variety of subjects including the necessity for nonprofits to diversify their portfolios based on certain standards. UPMIFA expressly addresses the needs of charities by providing for diversification and pooling of assets in a comprehensive manner that is consistent with modern practices in trust and not-for-profit corporation law.

Rules governing expenditure have been modified to give the institution's governing board more flexibility in making expenditure decisions, enabling them to cope with fluctuations in the value of the endowment.

States are still in the process of adopting UPMIFA. To see a current list of the States that have adopted this law, please check the following website: www.nccusl.org.

## Historic Dollar Value

UPMIFA eliminates the historic dollar value rule governing underwater funds—funds whose value, owing to the Great Recession, is below the original value of gifts at the time they were donated. Under UMIFA, institutions were not allowed to spend from a fund if its asset value was below its historic dollar value. UPMIFA replaces this with a more flexible spending rule, pursuant to which trustees may spend or accumulate as much of an endowment's fund—including principal or income, realized or unrealized appreciation—as they deem appropriate to meet the mission goals.

Trustees should take into account the intended duration of the fund, the fund's purposes, economic conditions, expected inflation, investment returns, and other resources such as the institution's investment policy.

Elimination of historic dollar value should encourage investment committees to establish a spending approach that is responsive to short-term fluctuations in the fund's value.

## Institutional Spending: The 7 Percent Rule

UPMIFA includes an optional limitation available for those jurisdictions desiring to place limits on institutional spending.

The seven percent rule provides a rebuttable presumption that expenditures exceeding 7 percent of a fund's total assets over a rolling three-year period are imprudent. Enactment of this rule is left to the discretion of individual state legislatures.

Spending more than 7 percent will not automatically render an organization in violation of UPMIFA. Its board may have to make the case to state regulators, explaining the prudence of its actions under the unique, prevalent circumstances. This standard of prudence does not apply to an appropriation for expenditure permitted under a law other than this act or the gift instrument of a charitable gift annuity, pooled income fund, or donor advised fund.

## Fiduciary Standard of Care

UPMIFA adopts the prudence standard of investment decision-making, requiring directors or others responsible for managing and investing the funds of an institution to act as a prudent investor. This includes using a portfolio approach considering risk and return objectives of the fund.

The above duties apply to:

- Directors of the institution
- Trustees
- Investment managers/agents, who have been delegated responsibility for management of funds
- Officers and employees of the institution

The above individuals are required to manage and invest funds in good faith and with care that a prudent investor would exercise. This language is derived from the Uniform Prudent Investor Act.

## Investigate/Verify Facts

UPMIFA notes that in managing and investing institutional funds, the institutions should only incur appropriate and reasonable costs. Costs should be reviewed in relation to the assets, purposes of the institution, and with respect to the skills made available in return.

Costs also include those incurred by the hiring of an investment consultant, which should be appropriate and reasonable under the circumstances.

Investment consultants and trustees should make a reasonable effort to verify facts relevant to investments and use this information in the decision making process.

Both these duties are consistent with the prudence standard under the act.

## Prudent Decision Making

Under UPMIFA, factors to be considered in investment decisions, unless otherwise provided by a gift instrument are:

- Economic conditions
- Effects of inflation/deflation
- Tax consequences

- Role of each investment in overall portfolio
- Expected total return from income and appreciation of investments
- Other resources of the foundation
- Distributions and the institution's need to preserve capital
- Asset's special relationship/value with the charitable purpose of the institution

Additionally, the institution's mission, current programs, and desire to obtain additional donations should be taken into consideration in determining appropriate investment assets.

## Portfolio Strategy/Risk and Return

According to UPMIFA, management and investment decisions for institutional funds should be made from a holistic standpoint, taking into consideration the institution's total investment portfolio, and weighing the risk, return, and objectives of the fund. Suitability standards should be applied to individual assets; however, an investment asset should not be viewed in isolation, but in conjunction with the overall portfolio.

This reflects the use of Modern Portfolio Theory (MPT) in investment practice. MPT explains how risk-averse investors can construct portfolios in order to optimize market risk for expected returns, emphasizing that risk is an inherent part of higher reward.

## Diversification

UPMIFA mandates that an institution's investment funds must be diversified, unless due to special circumstances, it is reasonably determined that the purposes of the fund are better served without diversification.

A decision to retain property must be made based on the needs of the nonprofit and not for the sole benefit of the donor. This decision may be made in the hope of obtaining additional contributions from a donor, therefore it may be considered as a benefit to the charity. The appropriateness will depend on the particular circumstances of the institution and its investable assets.

## IPS and Investments

The Investment Policy Statement should address the scope of investing. This includes the areas of investment that are allowed under the decision of the investment committee, largely based on asset allocation analysis, risk tolerances, and regulatory restrictions. More than simply specifying what an investment committee *can* invest in, this section should encompass all investment vehicles in which the nonprofit *cannot* invest.

An IPS should have a section covering the objectives and policies of the nonprofit. They are grouped because they often go hand-in-hand. The policies are the means through which the objectives are met, and they both need to be tailored to match one another. Defining the objectives of an organization's investments is crucial to the effectiveness of the IPS and the success of the nonprofit.

These objectives should include those that the investment committee and ultimately the board deem important enough to be included, and are typically listed in priority order. The range of topics comprising the objectives and policies section of an IPS can be far-reaching, but this section is important and is often the greater part of the IPS.

The objectives may be laid out to help meet the needs of the investment program like minimizing risk of sharp declines in value, maximizing returns, generating a selected level of income, and having assets exceed liabilities. Many components including liquidity, preservation of capital, stability of returns, long-term capital growth, annual returns, and current income must be considered to meet the needs of the nonprofit.

The financial objectives and policies section should also clearly specify the general aspects of the finances of the nonprofit and it should include the objectives and policies of the finances, control, asset protection, and major risks of a nonprofit. The elements that are often included, but certainly not limited to, are:

- *Reporting techniques*—most typically a quarterly report, including financial positions and financial operating results. This can be provided by a treasurer, but the investment consultant will also provide in-depth quarterly reports or reports with any reasonable frequency that the investment committee may require.
- *Debt payback methods and objectives*
- *Conflicts of interest to be avoided*

The overall purpose of the level of detailed information in this section is to ensure that the ongoing financial condition of the nonprofit is consistent with the priorities approved by its board.

## The IPS and Asset Allocation

Another section of the Investment Policy Statement covers the asset allocation policy determined through the Asset Allocation Analysis process. This portion of the IPS outlines, in great detail, the nucleus of a nonprofit's investment strategy. It states precisely what ratio of different investment vehicles the nonprofit will adhere to. As stressed earlier in the Asset Allocation Analysis chapter, this written guideline is of greatest importance when financial markets shift. It prevents the investment committee from making decisions based on emotional reactions to the market. Derailing a sound and reasoned investment strategy in response to short-term changes in the market is one of the worst investment decisions any nonprofit or investor can make.

The asset allocation strategy section of the IPS also outlines how to diversify the portfolio and provides documented proof that the organization has a plan. It outlines the risk tolerances and it is in the asset allocation strategy section of the IPS that the painstaking work of weighting the investment committee members and determining the optimal risk tolerance of the nonprofit will be realized. This is the conduit through which risk tolerance becomes more than a concept. The asset allocation section of the IPS brings theory into practice.

## The IPS and Risk, Return, and Money Manager Retention

The Investment Policy Statement also helps to reduce risk by including information and solutions around issues and potential problems that may arise internally, for which the investment committee and the organization should be prepared.

These issues can include:

- Loss of key personnel, such as any directors or investment committee members.
- Loss of performance or administrative facilities.
- Succession planning to establish what to do when investment committee members step down and end their tenure.

Establishing a reserve funds system suitable to the needs and goals of the nonprofit in order to effectively evaluate money manager performance, the Investment Policy Statement will establish specific return objectives in the various investment categories. Return objective discussions are typically intense and merit a detailed examination during the IPS adoption process. Whether one manager is retained or let go is greatly affected by the objective that was originally specified.

It is also important to keep in mind that no one metric will ever provide a complete picture. Therefore, the IPS should allow different types of measurements to be taken into consideration. These can include nominal and real return targets, a manager universe, a reference benchmark, or a primary benchmark. Including these other factors and benchmarks will provide the money manager with a means to more fully explain their performance. The key to this approach is for the investment committee to establish which metrics are best suited for the nonprofit. There are generally three considerations in terms of measurements. They must be:

1. Compatible with the money manager's investment style
2. Compatible with the nonprofit's investment goals
3. Properly prioritized

Evaluating return is relatively simple when compared to the next step, which is evaluating risk. It is one thing to establish the risk tolerance in the IPS, quite another to witness it in action. A money manager may employ a wide range of complex, statistical risk variables. Often they will have very little to do with the nonprofit's actual risk tolerance. Keeping it simple is generally best. For the investment committee, risk is usually measured in just two ways:

1. Achieving the targeted return
2. The likelihood of sustaining a significant loss over a specified timeframe

Finally, it is in considering the rate of return and matching it to objectives where the decision to retain a money manager is usually made. It is never easy, but a sound IPS will encourage a proper discussion relating to retention by setting appropriate evaluation standards known to everyone from the beginning.

## The IPS and Major Donors

It is important for investment committee members to keep in mind that there is tremendous awareness around nonprofit organizations having sound governance and fiduciary practices. Individual contributors have a whole new attitude and sense of entitlement around knowing what the nonprofit will be doing with his or her contribution and that includes knowing about the investment policy and philosophy. It is natural for a donor to pose the following question, "You've asked me for a lot of money, how are you going to invest it?" Donors are much more comfortable making sizeable donations when they have evidence substantiated through fact, documentation, and an explanation of the process by which decisions are being made. The existence of a sound Investment Policy Statement will provide documented proof of the sound governance and fiduciary practices and lay concerns to rest. Remember, the IPS should be unique, like your charity. Although there are standard elements included in an Investment Policy Statement, every nonprofit is unique and this should be reflected in the IPS. In theory, an IPS should be like snowflakes: no two should be identical. Some will be longer than others; some will be more dedicated to asset analysis, while others will pay attention to the inner workings of the nonprofit. What is most important is that the Investment Policy Statement is tailored to the precise needs of the organization.

## End of Chapter Review Questions

Here are some questions you should consider and answer after reading this chapter:

- Do you have an Investment Policy Statement (IPS)?
- If you have an IPS, is it current?
- Does your IPS contain all of the key elements discussed in this chapter?
- Do you adhere to the policy when making investment decisions?

## Summary

This section served to inform us of what the Investment Policy Statement is and how having a written document which outlines the procedures and processes that govern the management of a nonprofit's assets can be a critical component to success. We learned not only why these documents are so important, but also what elements within them are the most critical and how to ensure that an IPS is concurrent with legislation as well as our own fiduciary responsibilities.

Next, in Chapter 8, we discuss the money management selection process. We go over the details of both quantitative and qualitative analysis. And we use this information to relate back to our previous learning to construct a portfolio of money managers that meet our fiduciary obligations and our Investment Policy Statement guidelines, making sure they are in line with our risk tolerance and asset allocation guidelines.

# CHAPTER 8

# Money Manager Selection

For all our efforts to make a science out of investing, it still remains a very human process. The money managers are as important as the procedures and strategies adopted through the Investment Policy Statement. Not every money manager will be a good fit for every nonprofit investment portfolio. It is essential for the investment committee to have a thorough and detailed money manager selection process and the right investment consultant leading them through that process, enabling the committee to identify a money manager who is a good match for the nonprofit's investment strategy and objectives.

## The Goal

A mid-sized nonprofit will have six to ten money managers; optimally, each will possess an area of expertise and experience that suits the nonprofit's investment goals. The primary objective of the selection process is to obtain the best possible manager for each asset class with the expectation that the portfolio will obtain optimal performance.

The process of selecting the money managers can be time consuming and requires a great deal of focus. It is not as easy as determining which manager has the best track record. Every professional has good and bad periods, and it is no different for money managers. Given the manager's area of expertise, and state of the current market, their performance will fluctuate. The primary goal is to find the best person for the job, who may not necessarily be the top performer at the moment. To make this possible, no artificial constraints should be placed on the search. The investment committee must gather all pertinent information, be objective in evaluating it, and set aside emotions and bias during the entire process, especially during the final determination.

In order to make the selection process efficient, the investment committee must have well-established investment goals outlined in the Investment Policy Statement and access to a comprehensive database of money managers including details regarding their performance and specialized knowledge. The time and effort required to select the *right* money managers is essential in order to achieve the goal of meeting the Investment Policy objectives and ultimately the nonprofit's mission goals. The *wrong* manager can lead to a decrease in portfolio performance or an unacceptable increase in risk. It can also often lead to administrative difficulties and unnecessary expenses that are realized during an untimely release of a money manager.

## Outlining the Process

The first two steps in finding the right money manager consist of a comprehensive search followed by a careful evaluation of all candidates. The selection process will be driven by the criteria set by the investment committee in the Investment Policy Statement. A well-crafted IPS is essential for the search process to be efficient. Attention must be given during every step of the search and selection.

### Search Components

The essential components of a good manager search include:

- Clearly outlined goals and objectives in the Investment Policy Statement
- An objective review of a comprehensive database of money managers to define a complete list of appropriate options.
- Application of a set of well-defined, quantitative, and qualitative attributes.
- Focus on money managers who consistently follow the desired, and permissible, investment styles which they would be hired to pursue.
- Evaluation of factors beyond basic performance.
- Comprehensive comparative analysis of all managers by respective investment style.

### Search Criteria

Investment committees should be reviewing the following criteria for each potential manager:

- Investment style
- Investment class

- Experience
- Integrity and reliability
- Prior success in rate of return
- Decision-making process
- Consistency
- Time frames and the history of investment volatility within them
- Relevant resolution of legal issues if applicable

The judgment exercised by the investment committee members in these and other criteria is essential to a proper choice.

# Step 1: The Search

The first step in the actual search is to construct an extensive database of potential managers who fit the requirements of the nonprofit. Criteria are then applied to the database and mismatched managers are removed from the list. The next group of managers to be removed will be those who lack a desired investment philosophy, staff, plan, performance history, or infrastructure. At this point the list should be culled to a manageable number from which the analysis and selection process can begin.

The most common way to organize the list is by separating the managers by investment style, that being the style by which they manage their accounts. On the broadest level managers can be divided by those focused on fixed-income versus equities, then it is important to begin drilling down to the specific style specialization or capitalization focus. Some money managers focus on large market capitalization companies while others focus on mid or small cap. A manager may favor specific style security or discipline like value or growth. Many managers invest across several of these; for example, a value manager might invest across the entire market capitalization range, or a small cap manager may invest in both growth and value securities. Consideration should be given to the nature of the investments being domestic (U.S.), international, or global and finally, the investment committee will need to decide whether to invest with an active or passive manager and review the advantages and disadvantages of each. An active manager strives to surpass the market index, while a passive manager's goal is to match the market index. The criteria around the management styles and investment disciplines the investment committee considers during the search should be defined in asset allocation outlined in the Investment Policy Statement.

While it is important to know which style is associated with which candidate, the investment committee should keep in mind that managers change styles, and even when they don't, they often can't be identified with a single category. Consequently, attempts at pigeonholing money managers tend to be counterproductive. Given such limitations, identifying a money manager with a specific style is an aspect of the process that should not be overvalued.

Given the large number of options available, it should be evident that a sound Investment Policy Statement and clear asset allocation criteria are essential as key drivers in the search process. The complexity of the options and considerations also reinforce the importance of having the right investment consultant leading the investment committee through the process. It is a best practice for the Investment Policy Statement to clearly state that any outside consultant utilized by the investment committee to guide them through any portion of the money manager search process must not have a connection or affiliation with any of the money managers or money manager firms. The investment consultant should provide unbiased guidance through the search and subsequent evolutions. Both the search and the evaluation will be conducted and prepared confidentially to enhance their objectivity. The money managers under consideration will not even be told the name of the nonprofit considering them.

The investment consultant would typically take responsibility for gathering a list of appropriate money managers and may even provide value by sharing his or her personal experience working with one manager or another. The investment consultant's involvement certainly provides a tremendous amount of value to the investment committee; it saves time and energy as the investment consultant is intimately familiar with the process and can facilitate condensing the initial vast pool of money managers into a manageable number, ready to be evaluated.

## Step 2: The Evaluation

The second step in finding the right money managers is the evaluation phase that includes a lengthy consultation and thorough analysis of everything from the investment philosophy to the investment performance of the remaining contending managers. This process can be quite complicated, but the return on the time and effort is invaluable and will serve to effectively cull the list of possible money managers.

Evaluating the candidates begins with in-depth research around a wide-range of relevant information; this step is often the responsibility of the investment consultant. During this step in the phase, the investment consultant will explore specific criteria with the managers including how well the manager can articulate their philosophy, working style, performance, and economic views to an investment committee.

Additionally, the investment consultant is looking for consistency in a manager's past performance and return relative to the amount of assumed risk. If managers are inconsistent in their returns it is more likely that, even if they have performed well recently, you risk investing at the end of a hot streak and losing money. The basic historical performance of money managers is not the most prudent method for selecting managers; hindsight does not work as well in investing as it does in other aspects of life. Nonetheless, appropriate analyses of prior performance numbers will allow the investment consultant to guide the investment committee toward culling the list even further

## Investment Style and Benchmarks

Since money managers tend to associate with a specific asset category, comparing a candidate against the accepted benchmarks of the manager's asset category can be very helpful. However, while it is a means for establishing the level of risk identified with a specific manager, many experts caution against depending excessively on the benchmarks. Some money managers are unwilling to assume much risk and limit themselves to benchmark investments because they fear taking risks that might adversely affect their performance and make it more difficult for them to acquire new clients. These managers tend to be very conservative in their approach and while they are unlikely to perform below the benchmark, they are also not likely to exceed it significantly.

Others who deviate more often or aggressively from the benchmarks should not be judged too harshly if they have underperformed over short timeframes. These managers are working to provide a greater than average rate of return and the timeframe used for the comparison can skew results enormously.

Keep in mind that the benchmarks themselves are often changed over various timeframes, making direct comparisons more difficult and less reliable. It is also not unusual for the best money managers to manage portfolios for which no good benchmark is available. They bring their unique approach and style that may not be shared by the majority. It only serves to remind us that benchmarks are just one tool in evaluating potential money managers, and one that should not be overvalued.

## Step 3: The Analysis

The third step in the process is the analysis. Once the evaluation of the money managers is complete, the investment consultant should provide the investment committee with a detailed written analysis for each manager's investment style, rate of return, risk, and risk-adjusted returns. The report will include those issues, if any, which are the result of assessing the firm's structure and organization. In addition, the analysis will include appropriate benchmarks that can be used to evaluate the relative performance of the money managers and it will compare each candidate against a peer group of managers with the same investment style. The way the analysis is presented should facilitate comparison among the various candidate money managers.

Regardless of the number of money managers under consideration, the written analysis typically consists of seven categories, including:

1. *The Overview.* This details the screening process, describes how the pool was created, lists the objectives of the money manager evaluation, and offers a summary of those issues important to each candidate money manager's style, structure, and performance.
2. *Money Manager Vita.* This contains the money manager's profile, performance composite, and necessary descriptive information.
3. *Investment Style.* This includes the particular investment style and philosophy of the candidate money manager. It analyzes each money manager in consideration of their overall rate of return, including both return-based style analysis and fundamental style analysis.
4. *Return.* This lists the return the money manager has secured and compares it to the appropriate benchmark and money manager peer group. Included will be a comparison during various timeframes and under different market conditions.
5. *Risk.* Over a statistically significant timeframe, this considers volatility, overall market performance, and an analysis of various risk factors.
6. *Return to Risk.* Employing various accepted ratios, this includes a statistical analysis of the candidate money manager's return as compared to degree of risk.
7. *Evaluation.* This is a summary evaluation of the candidate money managers, providing a grade based on the comprehensive selection criteria that have been employed. It permits a peer ranking.

## The Mix and Number

Diversification does not relate strictly to the portfolio's variety of stocks and bonds. It also applies to the number and type of money managers it utilizes. Ideally, the nonprofit will want a mix of money managers with different, even contrasting, investment styles, philosophies, and a wide range of experience and expertise. A mix in gender, artificial as that seems, and in age can also be useful.

There is no magical means for selecting the optimal number. Six to ten money managers tends to be the average and works for most medium-sized nonprofits, but a smaller number of highly regarded managers can also be effective, as can a larger number with a greater degree of specialization. Most importantly, the mix and number should be manageable and measurable against the well-thought-out plan detailed in the Investment Policy Statement.

## The Measurements

The accepted industry-wide measurement and evaluation tools for money managers are Alpha and Beta, standard deviation, and the Sharpe Ratio.

*The Alpha* is the measure of a manager's excess performance relative to whichever index in which they focus their investments, then adjusted for the Beta. A positive Alpha means that the money manager is outperforming his index.

*The Beta* is a method of measuring the risk associated with a money manager. The Beta measures volatility in relation to the market index in which he or she focuses. The measurement is based around the foundation number 1.0. A Beta of 1.0 indicates that the manager's performance experiences the same ups and downs as the market, meaning that he or she is no more or less risky than the market. Any number greater than 1.0 means that the manager's portfolio is more volatile than the overall market in which it is invested, while a Beta of less than 1.0 indicates less risk than the index. It is important to also consider how the assets are invested when analyzing the Beta measurement.

Caution must be taken here because managers can alter their Beta numbers by placing some of their assets in cash or cash-equivalent investments, which lower the overall volatility of a portfolio, masking the existence of investments in high-risk securities.

*The standard deviation* of a money manager is similar to a Beta measurement, although it isn't quite the same. While the Beta measures against the overall investment market, the standard deviation only measures the performance of the single manager against him or herself. The higher the standard deviation, the more ups and downs a manager's performance experiences. The higher the highs and the lower the lows, the less appealing is a money manager. This relates back to his or her consistency.

*The Sharpe Ratio* measures the return of a manager per unit of risk. In this case, risk is defined as the standard deviation of the manager's return. Sharpe Ratios are most valid when comparing money managers that invest using the same style and market capitalization. The accepted practice here is that the higher the Sharpe Ratio, the better the money manager, as it indicates a higher level of relative return for the incremental risk being taken.

The investment consultant can apply the Sharpe Ratio analysis and other measurement tools in a peer analysis report in order to compare and measure the managers who have made it to this stage in the process. The peer analysis is important for several reasons. A money manager who has made it this far along in the process may be showing good numbers across the boards, have consistent returns, manageable risk, and high Alphas and Sharpe Ratios.

However, they may not be all that they initially appeared to be. It may be that with all of these positives, the money manager is, in fact, at the *bottom* of his or her peer group. They may have just been investing in the right style and not doing so as well as the others. For example, if large-cap growth is dominating the market and performing well, most managers who concentrate in that area will perform well. Because of that performance, they will not have been filtered out of the selection process. Peer group analysis comparing how everyone in that same investment class is doing will be very instructive. By conducting this peer group analysis, an investment consultant can weed out the managers who are in the right place at the right time from the managers who are in the right place at the right time *and* are also great money managers.

## Adherence to Investment Style

Does a prospective money manager consistently follow their professed investment style? Some money managers may just be tactically reallocating their portfolios to follow market trends, which is exactly the action an Investment Policy Statement seeks to avoid. Money managers who remain consistent to their investment discipline in changing market conditions are those to whom an investment committee will want to entrust the management of their portfolio.

   This is one reason why it is important to pay close attention to how well a money manager performs in different market cycles. In a bull market a bad money manager can make himself look good by producing sufficiently high returns to compensate for years of bad investing. And the opposite can also occur. It is necessary to understand the big picture and not be blinded by misleading money manager performance reports. If a money manager stays true to his investment style, and the investment committee understands that downs will inevitably appear on average about one-third of the time for very good managers, when dealing with quarterly results, then the committee can understand how a money manager fits into the investment program. There will always be downs in the market in short-term scenarios, and it's the superior managers who prove their worth by performing well time after time, relative to indexes. If investment committee members are aware of this, they will be able to decide which money managers are the best. Selecting a money manager who reallocates outside of his or her investment discipline can result in a derailing of the established investment objectives. This is a potential that can be avoided by selecting appropriate money managers.

## Operational Issues

The operational aspects of money management firms can have a great deal to do with how the money managers will perform in the future. How well does a firm retain great managers and officers? Analyzing a money manager is actually analyzing the performance of several individuals. If the key investment staff on the management team have been with the firm for many years it is likely that it was their work and performance that are being measured. If the management teams are constantly changing, hiring and firing lead investment personnel, it is likely that the committee will be analyzing the performance of someone who will not be managing its portfolio. Frequent changes in personnel in a money management firm usually spell trouble.

It is important to establish a trail of continuous performance to a specific money manager. If he or she is employed in a very successful firm, there is a tendency to assume he or she is responsible for that success, and you can be certain that is how it will be presented. But that might not be the case at all. The investment consultant can confirm that the specific money manager is taking credit for his or her own track record.

It is also important to know if a money manager receives research from the same sources employed by most of Wall Street, or if they conduct their own research. If they do not conduct their own research, then there is no advantage to that particular manager. For a management style that is uniquely successful, the money managers must be unique in their practices, including performing their own research. Another reason why conducting in-house research is so important for money managers is because buying information from other people may make things easier for the money manager, but it can add to the overhead of their operation, which in turn will increase the fees and commissions to investors.

The size of the money manager, ownership, and the length of time during which the manager has been operating are also very important considerations. The money management firms in which the owners are invested have a tendency to outperform managed funds that are run by employees because the owners have a stake in their managed portfolios. A money manager who has many years of market experience is obviously preferred over one who is new to the industry and may not be aware of all aspects of asset management. Also, firms that deal in large assets often have advantages over smaller firms. If there is a lot of money with them and they have been around for a long time, it is typically true that they have deep investment talent and have proven that their money management is a winner.

## Fees

Samuel Goldwyn, of the film studio, Metro-Goldwyn-Mayer, notorious for his malapropisms, is attributed as having said, "It is impossible to make predictions, especially about the future." The same could be true when

discussing predicting investment performance or the effectiveness of particular money manager. What you *can* know in advance is the fees you will be
asked to pay.

Fees require special attention. Just as small incremental improvements in
decision-making can have great rewards, so too will a slightly higher fee at
the start adversely affect the eventual rate of return. Some money managers
are worth their fees, others are worth less than they want.

The obvious hope is that the money managers the investment committee selects will deserve their fee; that is, that the money manager will
bring such value to their portion of the portfolio that the fees charged will
not seem significant. The law of supply and demand typically dictates fee
level, and there is little that can be done about that. The best at what
they do, as is the case in any profession, tend to be paid the most, and as
so often in life, when it comes to money managers, you usually get what
you pay for. But, committee members should keep in mind that there are
no guarantees. A high fee does *not* assure a greater than average rate of
return.

In most cases the money manager has a set fee schedule. However, if the
nonprofit's portfolio is large enough, fees can be negotiable. Fee negotiation
with money managers is a very specialized area and not one that lends itself
to a quick study. The investment consultant will either possess such expertise
or will call on someone who does.

Some investment committees lean toward performance fees in the hope
this will safeguard them from paying excessive fees for poor performance. It
is argued that performance fees are the most fair because the money manager
is compensated for his rate of return and in this scheme the organization does
not pay significant fees for poor performance. However, investment committee members should keep in mind that the organization will only pay a
lower fee if the rate of return is *below* the specified benchmark. In other
words, you pay less when you haven't gained much. Considered in that light,
they lose much of their appeal.

Performance-based fees are also subject to the criticism that they
encourage risk-taking during a specific timeframe when the money manager
has not done well. If during the grading period, say a quarter, the investments
have fallen well short, the money manager will be under pressure to take on a
greater risk in hopes of making a greater gain and recouping his losses. This is
not an advantageous situation for the nonprofit. Upping the stakes is a quick
way to lose in both gambling and the market.

The schedule for performance fees is also quite complicated. It must be
thoroughly understood. They will have the effect of driving investments.
Before committing to a performance-based fee schedule, the investment
committee should keep in mind that a money manager will already be
strongly motivated to perform well. They understand that keeping the

nonprofit as a client is dependent on their performance. They do not require artificial inducements to do their best.

Regardless of the system ultimately employed with any money manager, the committee should be certain to know, in advance, *every* fee the nonprofit will be called upon to pay. This is not an area for surprises.

In addition to investment management fees, the issue of trading costs should also be considered when evaluating money managers. The larger firms have more trading capability, which can lead to reduced costs on transactions that, in the long run, can make a significant difference on portfolio profits (or losses).

# Step 4: Selection

The final step in the process is the money manager selection. At this point the investment committee should have a concise list of several money managers that are performing very well and seem able to meet the requirements of the organization and the Investment Policy Statement. From this list the committee will hold a series of interviews, evaluate presentations, and conduct careful evaluations. Money managers will be eliminated and the list of candidates will become more refined.

If the committee is considering a final decision largely based on past performance, or more specifically, on the degree to which the money manager has exceeded the established benchmarks for his or her investment class, it is generally acknowledged that 3 percent above the benchmark, exclusive of fees, is world class performance. It is from such a relatively modest improvement over a benchmark that a portfolio will greatly profit. But it may be prudent to place greater weight on any or a number of the other factors that have been made available through the process.

In the end, this four-step process for selecting money managers provides investment committee members with the information and tools to meet their fiduciary responsibilities and ultimately make prudent investment decisions. The nonprofit will have the ideal money managers for its needs. Risk tolerances will be satisfied. Asset allocation objectives will have been met; diversification of assets will have been accomplished. In time return goals will be realized and the nonprofit will grow to the next level as detailed in the Investment Policy Statement. If the investment committee has done its homework so to speak; that is, if it has prepared the Investment Policy Statement, performed an Asset Allocation Analysis, and completed the other important steps *prior* to the actual money manager selection process, the manager picked often has less to do with eventual success than the fact that the preceding procedures and decisions have already taken place.

## End of Chapter Review Questions

Here are some questions you should consider and answer after reading this chapter:

- Do you have an efficient process for conducting your money manager search?
- Are you measuring all of the elements of risk and return affiliated with each manager?
- What is the process you use for eliminating a manager?
- Are you familiar with the operations of the money management firms?
- If you are an investment committee member, as a fiduciary, are you comfortable that your current process enables you to make prudent financial decisions?

## Summary

In this chapter, we detailed the processes and procedures that make for a prudent money manager selection. Even if an investment consultant will be facilitating this process it is important that board members and investment committee members alike understand it. It is a complicated process that is almost as much an art as a science. But this foundation knowledge is designed to provide the base upon which to build the skills and knowledge required to hire the money managers that fit the needs of your portfolio.

Coming up in Chapter 9, we discuss Dynamic Portfolio Optimization, an advanced iteration of Modern Portfolio Theory that should play a part in nearly all aspects of nonprofit asset management. Dynamic Portfolio Optimization should have an impact on asset allocation, money manager selection, investment policy drafting, and risk analysis. Needless to say, it is an important part of nonprofit asset management.

# Dynamic Portfolio Optimization

M odern Portfolio Theory (MPT) has changed everything when it comes to portfolio management. As mentioned earlier, the concept was first advanced in the 1952 paper, *Portfolio Selection*, written by the renowned Dr. Harry Markowitz. For the first time, it was possible for investors to estimate anticipated risk and the rate of return, and to measure both with statistical reliability. From this came a methodology for constructing portfolios to optimize market risk against anticipated gains, making clear that while risk is intricately tied to return, it can be managed within acceptable parameters. This was not only a novel concept, but also quite revolutionary.

Markowitz demonstrated how to create a properly diversified portfolio and conclusively showed that such a portfolio was likely to perform well. He proved that in equal circumstances the portfolio with *less* volatility would outperform one with *greater* volatility. In essence, modern portfolio management has its origins in these architectural principles.

## Before Modern Portfolio Theory (MPT)

As mentioned earlier in the chapter on asset allocation analysis, prior to MPT, it was accepted practice for investors to focus on assessing the risk/return characteristics of the individual investment vehicle they were considering. The investment approach was to identify those vehicles that offered the best likelihood for reward with the least element of risk. A portfolio was then constructed from these. On its face, this sounds perfectly sound and that's why it was the philosophy employed for so many years.

But in such a system it was possible, and often occurred, to construct a portfolio entirely from a single class of investments, such as U.S. Treasury Bonds. This happened because individually, each met the desired standard. Instinct suggested, however, that this was not a wise approach. Though each on its own looked good, the same economic factors could adversely affect each of them in the same way and hence the investments overall. But it was feared that spreading investments about, just for the sake of covering all bets, would produce poor results.

What Markowitz did was to devise the mathematics of what came to be called the *diversification effect*. He demonstrated mathematically that investors were better served by focusing on selecting a *portfolio* with the desired risk/reward characteristics they sought, instead of compiling a list of vehicles individually with those characteristics. He demonstrated with a high degree of accuracy that a sound investment policy was about the portfolio and not the individual investments. This change in emphasis was profound in its impact.

## Modern Portfolio Theory

At its core, MPT is a mathematical approach for determining the optimal asset allocation for an established degree of risk. To accomplish this, Markowitz required first that a rate of return be established, and standard deviation of various returns be devised. Then, a method for evaluating and monitoring the investment vehicles be put in place, often called a matrix. His mathematical equations then calculated the asset allocations that had the lowest standard deviation from the projected rate of return. In other words, it showed how to invest with the least amount of risk.

MPT provides a vast backdrop against which to understand the various interactions of return and risk that are systemic to all investments. It has utterly changed how every institution, including nonprofits, manages its portfolio. It is the force behind passive investment techniques as well as the various mathematical models that are today extensively employed in managing risk and assessing potential gain.

Perhaps the single most important consequence of MPT is the accepted investment principle that one must surrender perceived safety and assume a measure of risk to receive better returns. Markowitz showed the relationship between risk and return, and demonstrated how to maximize return with the lowest level of acceptable risk.

Prior to this, no such correlation was understood to exist. In fact, risk was to be avoided if at all possible. The idea was to find that magical investment with great return and *no* risk (if possible) then put all the eggs into that basket. Markowitz's concept of managed risk changed everything.

Markowitz's theory was advanced by the work of others over the following decades. In general, it became evident that it was possible to construct an optimal portfolio that provided the greatest return for *any* established level of risk. The essential concept is that investments should be monitored, measured, and managed at the portfolio level, not by specific investment. Investment vehicles should ideally be selected not on their individual merit alone, but rather for their place in the balanced portfolio.

## Problems with MPT

As revolutionary as MPT proved to be, certain shortcomings later became apparent. They are generally agreed to be:

1. *The lack of a standard methodology to establish the key data input.* This meant that every money manager, or other analyst, who claimed to be following MPT could devise his or her own creation by skewing the incoming data. Even adhering to the prevailing industry standards of the time was, in fact, nothing more than following the latest trend.
2. *The timeframe became skewed and unreliable.* The information initially relied on in establishing a portfolio through MPT is traditionally grounded in monthly and quarterly timeframes. But in MPT the analysis is reduced to a matrix, deviations, and averages, and these are not usually tied to the customary timeframe investors rely on.
3. *MPT is a buy and hold model.* As traditionally formulated, MPT does not allow the kind of routine adjustments that are now possible through our more sophisticated market analysis and technology. In essence, you establish a portfolio and hold onto it until you perform another MPT review. MPT simply lacks the flexibility that is now possible and, because it does, limits opportunities for marginal rate of return increases that can significantly mount over time.
4. *Normal distribution must be followed.* Any deviation from normal distribution in a MPT devised portfolio causes the asset allocation to skew. Again, it limits what has come to be regarded as standard flexibility in managing a modern portfolio.

## Advantages of Dynamic Portfolio Optimization

During the long decades since *Portfolio Selection* was first published, there have been many improvements building upon MPT and practice. Our understanding of the markets and of investment strategy has advanced considerably, and today we possess far more tools with which to analyze financial forces than ever before. There are a number of new investment management systems, but perhaps the most effective has come to be generically known as Dynamic Portfolio Optimization (DPO). This strategy has been demonstrated to provide a greater rate of return than more traditional models wedded to Markowitz's 50-year-old model.

As DPO has been increasingly recognized for the advantages it brings to the traditional MPT portfolio, several of these are of significance. DPO should:

- Consistently outperform the MPT models.
- Increase the probability that you will avoid a bear market.
- Make it more likely to discover those factors impacting your portfolio.
- Provide an overall greater rate of return.

In addition, investors employing DPO tend to have greater confidence in their portfolios. Using DPO, they are less inclined to make decisions for psychological reasons or to direct ill-advised and resource-consuming reviews and reports.

## Characteristics of the Post-MPT Portfolio

As resources and tools for financial investment increased in sophistication after the 1950s, the limitations in MPT became apparent. It was possible to do a better job of creating a portfolio strategy and in managing the portfolio itself. There are various approaches to accomplishing this, but each seeks to optimize, that is, to maximize the rate of return while maintaining the same degree of risk.

To accomplish this, changes from the Markowitz model were necessary, including:

- Preventing distribution from skewing asset allocations
- Limiting the number of initial inputs needed to construct the portfolio
- Automatically updating the inputs
- Allowing an alternate form of risk assessment
- Establishing traditional timeframe references of months and quarters
- Creating a more flexible, or dynamic, structure, which allows altering the asset allocations as needed

Systems for permitting these changes have long existed and have well-established track records of performance and reliability. One key principle for optimizing a portfolio is that the underlying anticipated rate of return for any investment vehicle will influence its value. This is not as complicated as it may first seem. It simply means that the dividend anticipated from a stock will affect the value of the stock. This is true for every investment in the asset allocation, though it is not always that easily calculated. This is simply another way of saying that each vehicle has a relative, rather than a fixed, value. And because relative values are always changing, opportunities are routinely coming available.

# The Efficient Portfolio

MPT limits, and in effect, controls, volatility by diversifying risk among the various classes of investment vehicles. This is enhanced by adding to the mix the investment styles of the money managers. In this way a portfolio can be assembled with a defined measure of risk, but the overall risk to the portfolio is less than for any one of the vehicles. In other words, volatility tends to cancel itself out while still producing a higher-than-benchmark rate of return.

In this model, diversification is more a factor of how the various vehicles perform in relation to each other than compared to the actual number of vehicles held. The principle behind diversification is to have vehicles with various characteristics. If asset classes are not interrelated they will tend to balance against one another.

The investment committee's goal is to create what is called an Efficient Portfolio. This is defined as one that provides the greatest gain for an established risk level. It is possible, in fact, to chart a line that connects the efficiency factors and visually demonstrates the degree of efficiency inherent in such a constructed portfolio.

# The Mean-Variance Model

In MPT, the standard approach is to establish the optimal asset allocations by basing them on investment return averages, the standard deviations derived from them and various correlation coefficients. These have been set by relying on historical patterns of performance. This mean-variance model, however, has four serious considerations:

- Using standard deviation as a measure of risk
- The impact of certain return distributions
- The large number of inputs that must be estimated
- The absence of a logical procedure to generate expectation inputs over an extended timeframe

Dynamic Portfolio Optimization, as an extension of the traditional MPT, addresses these concerns by providing:

- A downside risk measurement in place of standard deviation.
- The downside risk measure that deals with the problematic return distributions.
- Asset allocation that is directly tied to certain influencing factors such as interest rates, political concerns, and so on, to obtain the most desirable mix.
- An alternate system that significantly reduces the number of inputs.

The effect of these changes is to create new points as to when and how to adjust asset allocations. In this way, DPO provides a reliable navigation tool to manage the modern portfolio.

## Dynamic Asset Allocation and Market Timing

Some investors rely on market timing as the key component in managing their investments. They will switch most, even all, of their portfolio from stocks to bonds when the circumstances appear right, then back again when they change. History proves this to be an exercise in futility.

Dynamic asset allocation constructs a portfolio with more than two investment vehicles. It guides the investor in rebalancing the portfolio among the established classes. Such effective movements are essential for a more productive portfolio.

Consider the situation when it comes to the periodic rebalancing that every portfolio undergoes. The most common method is to simply return the portfolio to the percentages provided in the Investment Policy Statement. The investment strategy might be to have a portfolio balanced with 60 percent stock, 35 percent bonds, and 5 percent cash equivalents. Most money managers would simply blindly return to those numbers when a rebalancing point is breached. What he or she would be ignoring are the lessons of behavioral finance. People, even institutions, tend to behave at certain times with a herd mentality. This is also one of the reasons why all investment vehicles have a relative value. At such times, these relative values can mean that a certain asset class is under or overvalued. These are opportunities, opportunities the traditionally constructed and managed MPT portfolio cannot exploit. Responding to such opportunities is not the result of instinct, but is rather the consequence of well-established and detailed analysis with tried and tested methodologies. The investment consultant will either be knowledgeable about these or know the expert to consult who is.

What this leads to is tactical modeling. That is, though investments remain within the established parameters, a determination is made as to which assets are over or undervalued and the rebalancing is made with that taken into account. In the above example, the IPS would allow a range of percentages for stocks; say 50 percent to 70 percent instead of simply 60 percent. This allows for a more significant change in this asset class based on the knowledge of current market conditions and the relative value of the vehicles.

These methodologies in Dynamic Portfolio Optimization permit the exploitation of gain opportunities provided by market inefficiencies. They tend to be incremental and not dramatic, but applied systemically over time they add significantly to the portfolio's rate of return

## End of Chapter Review Questions

Here are some questions you should consider and answer after reading this chapter:

- What model are you using to evaluate your portfolio?
- What methodology do you use for rebalancing?
- Are you using Dynamic Portfolio Optimization methodology?
- Is your investment consultant providing you with tactical modeling suggestions?

## Summary

In this chapter, we discussed the use of dynamic portfolio optimization in the portfolio design and construction process. Dynamic portfolio optimization is a unique extension of Modern Portfolio Theory that seeks to expand on the ground-breaking theories of such great investment minds as Harry Markowitz. We learned what this system means to portfolio construction and how its approach to asset allocation, rebalancing, and expanded understanding of risk can improve portfolio results.

Coming up next in Chapter 10 we go over the process that is recommended for evaluating and maintaining a nonprofit investment strategy once it has been implemented. We discuss how to monitor accounts, including keeping tabs on money managers, as well as benchmark relative evaluation practices, peer group comparisons, and what can be done on a monthly, quarterly, and yearly basis to ensure that our portfolios are in line with our strategies and goals.

# CHAPTER 10

# Investment Program Analysis

O nce the investment strategy is in place and the portfolio decisions have been made and put into action, it is then necessary to monitor and analyze performance. Regardless of the superior nature of the overall investment program, monitoring is required to assure that it stays as intended and is responsive to the nonprofit's needs. This must not be an *ad hoc* procedure or one that takes place only when there is a perceived problem because by then it will almost certainly be too late and lead to ill-advised decisions.

An established process is designed to monitor every meaningful aspect of portfolio management in a routine manner. By monitoring and evaluating a number of significant variables, the investment consultant will usually anticipate problems sufficiently in advance to allow a more productive response by the investment committee. With a proper system in place, decisions will not be made by impulse or in a state of perceived crisis.

## Monitoring Accounts

Monitoring is meant to raise issues for review, but the results of monitoring will not always require that any action be taken. The primary purpose of monitoring is not to compel action, but rather to provide relevant information in a timely manner. It is the long lead-time this makes possible that gives effective monitoring its great strength.

A monitoring process is designed to accomplish at least two objectives:

1. Identify issues that might have an adverse impact on the portfolio and investment strategy.
2. Provide the relevant information so that issues can be properly evaluated and a suitable course of action, if any, can be undertaken.

Even with an outstanding Investment Policy Statement and superior money managers onboard, there always exists an element of uncertainty about any portfolio. It is, unfortunately, not possible to eliminate all worry. An effective monitoring program will help enormously in minimizing the degree of concern the investment committee will typically experience, especially during a volatile market period. It should allow timely answers to important questions and unexpected concerns.

Having the necessary information about the portfolio during times of stress can provide a great deal of assurance. Decisions made in such a circumstance are far more likely to be beneficial over the long term. Knowing you have a process in place that assures you will get timely information is the best hedge against uncertainty any investment committee can reasonably expect. A systematic portfolio and money manager monitoring system will possess certain specific features that ensure the investment committee will routinely receive the information it requires to perform its duties. In most cases that information is provided quarterly. It will include detailed reports and charts designed for monitoring your specific investment strategy, investment performance, and portfolio activity.

In addition to occurring at least quarterly, these characteristics include:

- Account monitoring
- Money manager monitoring
- Relevant benchmarks for comparison
- Information to facilitate comparison with appropriate benchmarks
- An overview of the existing market conditions and performance statistics for peer investments and groups
- An evaluation from the integrated financial resource consultant relating to the relevant collected data

## The Procedure

In most cases, though not always, the report and accompanying evaluation will be prepared directly by the investment consultant. As the consultant is unaffiliated with any of the money managers, the investment committee is assured that he is acting impartially.

Before the investment committee receives this information and these reports, the investment consultant should have analyzed them and calculated overall rate of return. Typically, the consultant will also have examined the various affected components and compared these against the specified investment objectives and the parameters that were previously established.

The evaluation will analyze single money manager accounts and combined accounts with several money managers. Comparison of money managers will be made side-by-side so the investment committee can appropriately evaluate performance. The evaluation will also facilitate comparisons of various money managers responsible for different aspects of accounts. The previously established benchmarks, or, where appropriate, historical benchmarks, are integral in allowing the evaluation of the relative performance of the various money managers. In evaluating style, performance, and risk, the benchmarks are the yardstick.

The performance of an individual money manager will be compared to that of a group of money managers with a similar investment style. Such information is essential in putting a specific money manager's performance in proper perspective when compared to existing market conditions and peer performance.

Once all the information is collected, it is best practice for the investment consultant to provide his or her evaluation to the investment committee along with the supporting information just as he or she did during the selection process.

Though much of this can be conducted internally, there will be occasions when the process could include the investment committee and the money manager. There are three services relating to accounts that must be performed on a routine and regular basis:

- *Monthly*—Each month, each account must be reconciled to ensure accuracy. The reconciliation should focus on every item that impacts the account's market value. It should include the current position, cash flow, transaction activities, and fees. The information will be carefully scrutinized for omissions, inconsistencies, errors, or peculiarities. All disparities will be adequately examined and a resolution reached. The necessary data from all this is then entered into the reporting system's database for use in the next quarterly report.
- *Quarterly*—Each quarter a detailed set of investment reportsshould be prepared which examine every significant aspect of each account. Copies are provided to the investment committee and any others in the nonprofit's management who should have them for review and consideration. The investment consultant will then meet with the investment committee or its designated representative for such matters, if any, to discuss and evaluate the performance of the various accounts.

  As part of their responsibilities, in best practices, the investment consultant will have already conducted their own internal review of all accounts at least each quarter. The Consultant may draw on the expertise of certain consultants as needed and monitor each account's performance in light of the established parameters. They would make a note of inconsistencies or abnormal patterns and document their analysis. All of this will go into their evaluation that will accompany the quarterly report to the investment committee.

- *Annually*—Each year the investment consultant should reexamine the nonprofit's Investment Policy Statement and review the allocation of every account and its market position, as well as any changes in investment practice that may have occurred during the year. At an appropriate time the consultant should meet with the investment committee and discuss whether modifications to the IPS should occur. If that is agreed, the consultant should draft a formal modification for adoption and inclusion.

## Assessing Money Managers

While it is critical to assess regularly the performance of the portfolio, it is just as important to analyze the performance of the various money managers. It is routine best practice for the investment consultant to deal directly with each money manager on various aspects of his or her performance to facilitate the monitoring process. In such an approach the due diligence of monitoring money managers evolves as a joint responsibility of both the investment consultant and the investment committee.

Each money manager is periodically asked to confirm the accuracy of the information maintained about him and his company. The manager will also be asked to provide their most recent promotional materials, fee schedules, and management agreements. Such requests are often accompanied by a letter asking that each money manager answer a series of questions about any events or changes that may have an impact on the money manager.

Each month, if variances between the parameters and the account's position are observed, the investment consultant, should identify the aberration to the money manager for correction. If performance varies, they will typically contact the money manager, usually face to face, to discuss the continuing discrepancy. One avenue of discussion will be to consider if the parameter requires adjustment in light of the current market. If that is the case, the issue will be discussed with the investment committee or its representative. If not, the money manager should advise of the steps he or she intends to take to bring the account back into compliance.

On a daily basis, if required, the investment consultant should have discussions with the money manager around any issue concerning investments that have come up in order to reach an agreement on what should be done. In these cases, timely action usually produces the most positive result.

Finally, before the investment consultant meets with the investment committee on an account, he or she should have consulted directly with the appropriate money manager. While due diligence is always an aspect of their relationship, it is most effectively obtained in a cooperative environment and one in which regular communication takes place.

## Benchmarks

The purpose of establishing benchmarks as part of the investment strategy is to provide a yardstick against which to measure the performance of asset classes and money managers. It often occurs that other historical benchmarks must be compiled to allow proper monitoring and evaluating of money manager performance.

Benchmarks permit analysis to take place on a relative basis. Benchmarks form an integral part of the report on money manager performance, as they do on the performance on style and of asset classes. Benchmarks not already established are determined by analyzing a specific money manager's investment style along with the investment goal of the accounts. These must be properly balanced.

The analysis of a money manager's investment style has two components that should result in a consistent form of measurement:

- Examination of the core data of specific investment vehicles that the money manager has in his or her average portfolio.
- Examination of the related coefficients tracking the performance between the various performance measurements and the money manager's historical performance.

A certain benchmark may have but one index or it might be composed of a blend of several. This can mean tracking hundreds of indicators. In addition, every account will have total return benchmarks. In an account balanced with different asset classes, say, equity and fixed income, each will be assigned its own specific benchmark. The overall account, however, will receive a benchmark that has been custom designed and which reflects the account's target asset allocation. It should be noted that such a customized benchmark is *not* routinely rebalanced so it accurately reflects the existing asset weighting. This allows a comparison between the produced results from the investment strategy and the actual asset allocation.

In addition, it is necessary to have a benchmark for each matching portion of the portfolio. There will be a primary benchmark against which the money manager's performance is evaluated. There will also be a reference benchmark that is usually composed of a wider index and is not ordinarily specific to any certain investment style. Its purpose is to allow comparison of the money manager's performance against the broader market. There will be other benchmarks, such as one to measure inflation, which is of particular use in evaluating the bond portion of a portfolio.

The types of benchmarks and their number will vary from account to account even within the same portfolio as they must reflect the money manager's style and goal of each specific investment account.

## Peer Group Analysis

While comparing specific money manager's performance to a commonly accepted benchmark is of great value, it is also highly desirable to compare his or her performance against that of the peer money managers who administer similar accounts in related nonprofits. This peer group pool will also possess the same, or very similar, investment styles, and will match favorably with the style-specific indicators previously selected to be his or her account's benchmark.

In forming a peer group pool, the data relied on is taken from composite performance figures provided to commercial databases by various money managers. Only money managers who have reported their historical gross investment performance for at least the last five years are considered. This assures that the information is current and that data exists which can be applied for the comparison. This data is used to select for the pool those money managers who are favorably matched. This is an extensive process often involving more than 1,000 money managers in 4,500 investment composites. Individual performance composites are then divided into asset classes. Each asset class is subdivided into more specific groups that can be employed for comparison.

Once this has been completed, performance is then calculated for each money manager grouping within the pool. In addition, a calculation is made for all of the money managers, who are then ranked from highest to lowest each quarter. This provides the actual metric against which the individual money manager is compared.

## Investment Style

The money manager was retained with the expectation that he or she would manage the assigned account with a certain style; so evaluating a money manager's performance against investment style is essential. It will reveal if he or she is buying investment vehicles consistent with his or her history and stated style. It will also allow you to know if the money manager is remaining within the indicated investment parameters. If the money manager deviates from his or her style, and they usually do, it will impact the diversification, investment risk, and attainment of the account's objectives.

In examining a money manager's investment style, the investment consultant would typically employ a Holdings Based Analysis. This relies on the basic, or fundamental, characteristics of the specific vehicles that are in the account. In the case of equity securities, these include price, earnings ratio to price, book ratio and price, cash flow ratio, and the like. Duration, quality, and maturity are considered in the case of fixed-income vehicles such as bonds.

The second level of analysis is called Return-Based Analysis. This approach relies on the historical investment performance previously garnered. In other words, how does the previous rate of return compare to the rate of return for the current investment style? Return Based Analysis disregards the basic characteristics of all of the account's individual investment vehicles.

Though quite different, both of these analyses are important in determining how the individual money manager is positioning the account within the portfolio and how the portfolio itself is placed within the market as a whole. It is possible, however, that each approach may produce a very different answer. Their conclusions may yield inconsistent results. The significance is not that they elicit inconsistent outcomes, but rather that they raise appropriate issues that should be considered and possibly brought to the attention of the affected money manager.

## The Evaluation

The right mix of money managers is essential to the proper performance of the portfolio. The wrong mix will almost certainly lead to a failure to meet the targeted rate of return. But replacing money managers when it isn't called for is also disruptive and creates its own set of problems, not the least of which is increased expense unrelated to better performance. For these and other reasons, the evaluation of money manager performance must be comprehensive, fair, and informative.

Very similar to the initial money manager selection process, the investment consultant should gather as much relevant information as possible and draw comparisons when they are called for. The purpose isn't to give a specific grade score or to point the investment committee toward a single tactical decision. The consultant will collect and present what is needed so that issues requiring attention are identified in a manner that allows for timely and meaningful decisions.

The review and evaluation also serve an important function in assisting the investment committee to fulfill its institutional and individual fiduciary responsibilities. The point has been made several times and should be obvious that the investment committee's fiduciary responsibility is to uphold prudent investment management practices and a big part of that is having sound policy and practice around investment review. Additionally, as a final point, it is important to stress that although performance is extremely important, the key consideration to keep in mind when reviewing the analysis and performance is that the overall objective is to meet the mission goals and objectives of the organization, not necessarily to outperform the market.

## End of Chapter Review Questions

Here are some questions you should consider and answer after reading this chapter:

- What is your process for monitoring and analyzing performance? Is it detailed, documented, and adhered to?
- Do you have an impartial party preparing an evaluation and report?
- Is the report complete including all aspects of review:
  - Account monitoring
  - Money manager monitoring
  - Relevant benchmarks for comparison
  - Information to facilitate comparison with appropriate benchmarks
  - An overview of the existing market conditions
  - Performance statistics for peer investments and groups
  - Evaluation report, including an analysis of the relevant collected data
- Are you clear about the benchmarks and peer groups you should be measuring against?
- Are you meeting your mission goals with your current investment and spending strategy?

## Summary

In this chapter, we went over the evaluation and maintenance process for a nonprofit investment strategy once it has been implemented. We discussed what is involved in monitoring accounts, including continuing money manager due diligence. We also discussed benchmarking and peer group analysis and laid out what can be done on a monthly, quarterly, and yearly basis to ensure that our portfolios are in line with our strategies and goals.

Next, we discuss socially responsible investing.

# CHAPTER 11

# Socially Responsible Investing

*Using Investments to Generate
More than Monetary Gains*

Socially responsible investing (SRI) is a unique approach to melding mission and investing. In its most basic sense, SRI is an additional set of guidelines used to control the investment direction of a pool of assets, specifically guidelines which follow a moral or ethical doctrine. There are a number of reasons why organizations implement SRI strategies, how they implement these strategies, and what these strategies are.

In this chapter we explore not only how to implement these strategies, but why these protocols are important to an organization, the history of SRI investing, and the effects of SRI as we have witnessed them over the last several decades.

## The Roots of Socially Responsible Investing

In order to better understand SRI, we must first explore its roots. Looking back, the concept of SRI has existed for centuries. The Catholic Church for example has had extensive funds for centuries with which it has not only expanded itself and its goals, but invested in companies which fit into its religious tenets to promote its growth while building their own wealth. And of course today, the Catholic Church and many organizations under its auspices carry on with a number of SRI schemes and guidelines which have set them apart as one of the leading organizations for the SRI movement.

Religion for a very long time was the tap root of SRI. The colonization of America and early American life can be attributed in some way to SRI. After having sought their religious freedom, the Quakers prohibited certain business activities, such as slavery, which is in a sense, SRI. And one of the basic tenets of some of the founders of the Methodist movement was that an individual's business practices were tolerable only if they did not harm their neighbor—which could have been done through poor conditions for workers, pollution, or the creation of toxins, and so on.

In the modern sense of the term, SRI has really been around since the 1960s and has its roots in modern American investing. Just as 1960s America saw a great shift in social conscience with the civil rights movement, and women's liberation as well as strong developments in labor issues and the growing unrest surrounding the Vietnam Conflict, there was also a shift in how investment could be a part of changing the social and economic landscape of our country. Through this time of great change investors also began to view their wealth as a means of affecting change. This could be accomplished by not investing in the stocks of those companies that violated the standards of investors, a sort of equity boycott. Investors also sought to become activists on certain companies, trying to directly impact those practices that they found to be unacceptable. But we will get into the details of *how* to go about SRI later in this chapter.

The next great leap in SRI came in the 1990s, again focused largely around the United States, but also having a global focus and scale. At this stage in American history a great wealth had been created by the minds and work ethic of the World War II generation and the Baby Boomers who followed. Encompassed in this generation was a large group of people who had been at the center of the cultural revolutions of the 1960s, and now in addition to their beliefs, they had wealth—wealth with which to affect change. Coinciding with this fact was the emergence of a much broader and grander focus on the environment with issues such as global warming— or climate change—and pollution becoming a major concern for many people around the world. It is really during this period that the concept of SRI becomes a formal concept. Investment firms begin to make it a focus of their business and investors begin to consider their portfolios as more than just a means of generating return. They now view their portfolios as a privilege and a responsibility through which they can continue to make a difference like they did in the 1960s.

The burgeoning of the Internet age has provided a significant thrust to the growth of the SRI movement. Companies are now more liable for their actions as the news cycle has become 24 hours, almost everyone with an internet connection has a means of getting a message out to the world at large, and the advent of social media have put corporations under more scrutiny than ever.

The growth of the concept has been on a booming trajectory ever since, with the creation of new SRI products, new methods and means of screening investments, great increases in shareholder activism, and companies realizing that they have to get on board with this to keep their pool of potential investors as large as possible. In fact, according to a report published by Thomson Reuters, approximately one dollar out of every eight invested through a professional investment management product (meaning mutual funds, exchange traded funds, or separately managed accounts) is in some way involved in a SRI screening process or other means of SRI. An impressive fact when one takes into consideration the size of the professionally managed segment of the market, estimated to be more than $25 trillion.

Now that we have grazed the surface of how SRI came to be, let us begin to delve further into how it can be a part of your organization and what your nonprofit can do to get more out of its portfolio then just returns.

## What Exactly Is Socially Responsible Investing?

Socially responsible investing can take on many forms, and in this section, we will delve into some of the most common forms of SRI. We will delve into some of the details of terms like religion-based SRI, Environmental, Social, Governance (ESG), sustainable investing, and mission-based SRI. These are all unique forms that SRI can take, each of them share many characteristics, but all have different meaning to those who ascribe to their guidelines.

As discussed, one of the earliest and most common forms of SRI is that which is based upon a religion. Most, if not all, religions include a set of guidelines designed to act as rules or a moral compass for how to live one's life. Whether the driver behind that is to attain Nirvana, a place in Heaven, or simply to make the world a better place for those who inhabit it is essentially irrelevant for the purposes of this book. However, it is important that we not forget the root cause of this movement. Many religious groups in this country have nonprofit organizations with funds attached to them which are in place to further their own causes. While the crux of these pools of assets is to be spent on the organization or on other missions of the organization, many of those involved in the management of these realized that at the same time as growing their assets to increase their potential spending, they could be using those assets themselves to impact their causes. There are a number of different religious causes commonly utilized in the process of developing SRI guidelines. To provide some insight into just how expansive this segment of the movement is, here is a sampling of this list from some of the major institutional religions in this country:

- Abortifacients
- Contraceptives
- Weapons of war
- Alcohol
- Gambling

- Tobacco
- Pornography

Moving beyond religious nonprofits, there are also many other non-profits that maintain SRI guidelines on their portfolios one way or another to further thru mission. The genesis of this process is not necessarily based on a religious tenet, but rather based on the founding principles of an organization. For hypothetical example, if a nonprofit exists for the promotion of saving the rain forest, it might set a restriction on its portfolio to not invest in any companies that are known to participate in deforestation. Or, an organization involved in providing health care to its constituents might prohibit the investment of its funds in any company that might harm that cause, such as a tobacco company. Most nonprofit organizations have a stated mission and more and more often we are seeing nonprofits allow that mission to guide not only their grant making and activities, but also their investments.

In addition to these two facets of mission-based investing; there is also a growing interest in a type of SRI known as Environmental, Social, Governance, often referred to as ESG. This is becoming a very common means through which organizations determine their SRI mandate. ESG encompasses many of the guidelines that would be placed on a religious-based SRI mandate, a Sustainable mandate (as will be discussed later), and even covers the mission-based SRI mandates of a wide range of nonprofit organizations. The ESG mandate says it all in the title. It seeks to avoid companies that do harm to the environment while preferring those who follow sustainable practices. ESG also seeks to avoid companies that might harm society in any way, whether through harm to consumers through its products or harm to the world at large through the creation of weapons of war or products with immoral content. Under the Governance portion of ESG, investors who follow this mandate seek to avoid companies with corrupt or overpaid corporate management or those companies who exhibit patterns of employee mistreatment.

Sustainable investing is yet another popular iteration of SRI. The growing popularity of this facet of SRI is deeply rooted in the growing awareness and subsequent concern about the environment of our planet and what human activity is doing to it; the increase in carbon emissions first brought about during the industrial revolution and leading into the growing emissions of booming Emerging Market economies. Additionally, the unchecked expenditure of earth's finite resources is another area of great concern for many investors. Some of the top concerns for these investors are deforestation and the use of fossil fuels, natural fertilizers, fresh water, and arable land. In an attempt to direct the future heading of our planet, many investors are now using their portfolios as a tool to affect change in this regard. This can include avoiding investing in those companies which continue to pursue unsustainable environmental practices or which take action that is a detriment to the future of the planet. Or, in more and more cases investors are beginning to focus on providing more and more investment to those companies which are taking it a step further than simply doing no harm, but rather are attempting to better the planet through sustainable practices which actually improve the earth's resources. The advent of carbon credits, carbon offsetting, and being carbon neutral are all born of this set of ideals and many corporations are making moves in these areas of the market in an attempt to attract the types of investors that follow a Sustainable SRI mandate.

## How Do We Accomplish Socially Responsible Investing?

Now that we have explored some of the history and motivations behind why many individual investors and organizations follow SRI mandates, let us explore how to go about implementing portfolios that follow these guidelines.

The first and most obvious of these methods is probably also one of the oldest. This is the negative screening method. Simply put, a specific restriction for a specific SRI guideline would be placed on a portfolio. For example, a "no tobacco" guideline might be an SRI restriction for a particular organization portfolio. To enact this restriction, the organization would simply apply the screen on their portfolio for any stocks of companies that are in the business of producing tobacco or tobacco-related products. And any stocks that show up on that screen would be prohibited from purchase for the portfolio. Delving further into the negative screen method there are a number of means through which to apply this screen. Taking our tobacco stock example, an organization might want to further define this restriction. Perhaps they allow a slight leeway provision in their SRI guidelines, mandating that a stock will only be screened out on the basis of a tobacco restriction if it generates a certain percentage of its revenue from the sale or production of tobacco-related products. Or, moving in the other direction, an organization might put in place a zero tolerance restriction on a specific SRI screen. In this tobacco example that might include taking it a step further and reviewing the retail sales sector of the market and screening out any companies that sell tobacco products.

Although the negative screen is certainly the most common and easiest to implement form of SRI, there are a number of other methods that continue to grow in popularity as nonprofits and investment firms alike shift more of their resources into this growing market space. One of the most impactful forms that we have seen continue to grow is that of shareholder activism. This is exactly what it sounds like. Rather than avoiding owning stock in a particular company because they go against the mission or guidelines of an investor, they specifically buy shares in that company in an attempt to affect change, as a shareholder of common stock an organization has certain rights within the company. Those rights include the ability to write shareholder letters and participate in votes on shareholder actions. As voting shareholders, they also have the ability to vote on board changes which can have a major role in the direction a company takes. One of the main reasons for the recent increase in this type of SRI screening is the rise of the mindset that simply ignoring the negative actions of some companies is not enough for many nonprofit boards, they want to take it further and create change.

## The Risks of Socially Responsible Investing

Any investment prospectus will tell you; investing involves certain risks. Well, the same is certainly true for those interested in SRI. There are several different schools of thought on the various risks and rewards of SRI. Here we will open the discussion on what these tradeoffs might be, but every nonprofit is a unique investor and as such your organization and your board will need to carefully consider these potential risks as you begin to explore SRI.

One of the greatest sources of contention among analysts who study the effects of SRI on a portfolio of assets is the most basic question that will be the first in most people's minds: "Will excluding certain companies detract from my portfolio performance?" The answer is not as easy as a simple yes or no. In fact, there is enough contradicting evidence that it is uncertain as to whether or not there even is a correct answer at this time. On one side of the argument, proponents of SRI will argue that those companies who have sustainable practices, treat their employees well, don't harm their customers or the planet, and so on, will be the companies that over the long term have greater success. The logic here being that although cutting corners on employee benefits might increase the short-term bottom line and increase equity performance, it is unlikely that these practices will be sustainable. Therefore, those companies which are, for lack of a better term, "sinners," will eventually begin to underperform those companies which go the extra mile to do the right thing by their consumers, their employees, and the world at large.

On the other side of the table is the argument that in the worlds of business and investing, the only thing that matters is bottom line. Although that philosophy might strike some as cold and calculating, there is an argument to be made in favor of being just that when it comes to money. This ideal holds that an investment portfolio is designed to generate returns, creating more money for a nonprofit to directly put toward its mission. The utility of a dollar gained from an investment the belief goes, is more valuable on the nonprofit's balance sheet than a dollar invested in a company that is aligned with a nonprofit's mission.

As stated earlier, there is research out there to support both of these stances. However, it is our contention that an organization needs to carefully consider the possibility that both of these opinions may be right and therefore needs to carefully weigh the potential pros and cons of SRI investing during the initial phases of deciding if and how to implement this type of strategy.

Another risk to SRI is one less often thought of, but is still one that should be considered by boards and investment committees alike as it may have an impact on the organization. That risk is created by the fact that although an SRI mandate is almost always self-imposed on an organization, once it has written it into its Investment Policy Statement and advised its donors and constituents of the mandate it is obligated to follow those guidelines. Therefore it creates the risk of either missing something in its screening, not having a robust enough screening process, perhaps inadvertently purchasing a stock, or accepting a stock donation that is a violation of SRI policy. Although it is unlikely that this could not be remedied quickly once detected, the risk lies in donors and constituents learning that an organization has both violated its IPS and violated the trust of the donors by investing in companies that they had understood to be off limits. This could hurt future donations and cause harm to the reputation of an organization.

The third risk that we will discuss that goes along with SRI is that of limiting your investment universe. Although it might seem obvious that the universe of allowable investments would shrink with the implementation of an SRI policy, what we actually mean here is limiting the products and capabilities of a portfolio. For example, a commingled investment like an open-ended mutual fund, common in many portfolios, cannot be customized to suit a specific organization's need. Additionally, even if at the time of purchase it is not a violation of SRI policy, there will most likely not be anything in the fund's documents or prospectus that prevent it from violating the policy in the future.

Additionally, investments that fall into the category of what is broadly known as *alternative investments* provide no control over investments and little to no transparency as well. These investments can include hedge funds, managed futures, and private equity to name a few. And although there are very few investments in this market space that afford organizations the ability to follow an SRI mandate, they can play a critical role in the performance and diversification of a nonprofit's portfolio. The historical low or negative correlation of these asset classes can be an important part of risk management and portfolio construction. Therefore, many organizations allow for these by including a proviso in their SRI policy document that exempts these investments from their screening and SRI mandate. In addition to eliminating these types of investments there is a third group of investments that is the fastest growing in the investment world over the last several years and that is indexing. Indexing is typically accomplished through exchange-traded funds (ETFs) and has the same issues as those listed earlier. There are several ways around this, including a proviso that exempts a portion of the portfolio allowed to be indexed. Another option is the use of a separately managed custom index, which is designed to deliver the same market exposure as an index ETF, but allows the investor to implement a custom approach. And finally, there are a number of SRI based indices that can be purchased in ETF or mutual fund format. Of course, for these to work for a nonprofit the product would have to align closely or exactly with their respective SRI policy.

## Additional Means of Accomplishing SRI

There are a number of alternative methods of creating a portfolio that is socially responsible beyond those traditional methods that first come to mind when we hear the term SRI.

### De Minimis

The first we discussed earlier, and that is through shareholder activism. This is the process of owning a de minimis position in particular companies that would normally screen out of an SRI portfolio and owning them in an attempt to affect change at the company. When we hear the term shareholder activism we typically think of large professional investors like George Soros or Bill Ackman. These investors are typically buying large positions in companies to give themselves voting rights and affect change in a company that increase the value of the stock. The driver here is typically profit rather than positive social change (although that is not to say that the two are mutually exclusive—they very often go hand-in-hand). However, that is not the only type of shareholder activism. As we mentioned earlier, investors can try to impact an organization as a smaller shareholder, through the process of attending annual shareholder meetings, writing letters, and voting on corporate actions.

### Microfinance

Another form of SRI that is not something we think of in the traditional sense is through microfinance. Microfinance, also known as microloans, is using a pool of assets to provide loans on a small scale. This financing is typically provided to groups that make use of the assets in a socially responsible manner. This can include making a loan to a small village to provide them with land for growing food, fertilizer for growing food, research to provide water, or expanding electricity and waste disposal. In this regard the money is loaned out, often in relatively small denominations, with the intention of making an interest rate on the assets (as though your organization had purchased a bond) and the betterment of the recipient of the loan allows that group or individual to make these periodic payments or lump-sum payment depending on the terms.

This method can also be used to make loans to small nonpublic companies which are doing unique work that either fits well with a non-profit's mission or is socially responsible in that it is designed to make the world a better place for some group of people or some other cause that might align with your SRI mandates. Microfinance might sound daunting, but there is a growing group of organizations that are providing microfinance opportunities to nonprofit investors of varying types and asset sizes. We believe that this trend will likely continue to grow as it is not only often a very good investment, but also allows the investor to see the direct impact of their investment dollars.

## Why Does a Nonprofit Implement an SRI Portfolio?

There are a number of drivers behind the implementation of an SRI mandate on a portfolio for a nonprofit organization. The first and most obvious is to further enhance the mission of an organization. Nonprofits are all created and funded with a purpose, many of which is to serve to make the world a better place. It is a logical step that there is more to funding projects and making grants. An organization can use its assets to impact companies and their practices around the globe. Additionally, it is a means of both attracting donors and keeping current donors happy.

## End of Chapter Review Questions

Here are some questions you should consider and answer after reading this chapter:

- Does an SRI mandate make sense for your organization? Consider the risks discussed this chapter.
- If you currently have an SRI policy, is it clearly documented in either your Investment Policy Statement or a separate SRI document?

*(continued)*

- Have you reviewed your portfolio against a similar portfolio or benchmark that does not implement these screens? If so, how does it compare?
- If you have an SRI policy, do you have the proper structure in place to review and confirm compliance with the policy? Do you have a leeway provision allowing for a period of time for a violation to be remedied?
- Have you considered all of the different forms of SRI, like those discussed in this chapter?

## Summary

In this chapter, we learned a little bit about the history of socially responsible Investing and its evolution over time into its current form. We discussed what exactly SRI is and why organizations implement these policies. We discussed the different methods of going about implementing these policies as well as some of the risks associated with them. We discussed SRI not only for equity investments as they are typically thought of, but indexing, alternative investment, and commingled funds as well. We went over some of the drivers behind SRI including religious reasons, mission-based, ESG, and sustainable investing. We also discussed some alternative methods of SRI beyond traditional negative screening such as microfinance and shareholder activism.

Our goal here was to understand what SRI is and what it can mean for your organization. It is an important consideration and can play a major role in how your portfolio is run as well as a number of other areas of your nonprofit. Each organization places different emphasis on this and it requires careful consideration before either implementing or even deciding to avoid. It can be a great means of psychic revenue for not only your organization's staff and board, but for your constituents and donors as well, and psychic revenue is often a very valuable asset.

Coming up next, we discuss strategic development initiatives and how this important facet of nonprofit management can make an impact on your organization. We review some of the strategies and psychology involved in creating new donor pools, as well as expanding those already in place.

# CHAPTER 12

# The Changing Landscape for Fundraising

The prior chapters reflected on the effects the distressed economy has had on endowment values and the strategies and solutions—investment tools, policies, and procedures—nonprofit organizations should adopt to avoid getting caught off guard in the future. Yet depressed endowment values have not been the only issue putting pressure on nonprofits. The rules of the road to successful fundraising results have changed. Demand for programs and services has risen exponentially, giving patterns have changed, and donors are more discerning. All of these factors have created a new reality for nonprofits and a need for a Strategic Development Plan.

## Our New Reality

Across the country, we have seen insurmountable increases in basic needs. Studies show that in 2011, 90 percent of organizations that identified themselves as providing critical lifeline services noted an increase in demand;[1] 88 percent project demand will rise again. This is following three consecutive years of rising demand for services across the sector. Rising demand for service obviously works in tandem with rising need for funding. And with the market value of endowments dropping fewer dollars were being generated for programmatic and operational support.

To meet the increasing needs, organizations have had to increase their programs and services, and in turn, their spending, leaving us with another startling statistic: 57 percent of nonprofits have three months or less of

---

[1] "Convio Predicts Key Trends For The Nonprofit Sector In 2012," Convio, January 4, 2012, www.convio.com/convio/news/releases/convio-predicts-key-trends-for-2012.html.

cash on hand and 87 percent say their financial outlook won't get any better in 2012.[2] To exacerbate the problem, revenue wells are drying up and donors of all types have altered their giving. Government funding has been declining and unreliable at best. Organizations receiving commitments for government funding are waiting three, six, nine months for the money to arrive! With most holding less than three months in cash reserves, this delay causes a very serious problem.

Earlier in this book, it was mentioned that inflation-adjusted individual giving rates in 2011 only grew by 0.8 percent;[3] this dollar figure represents a flat stream of revenue for the nonprofits. In addition to the challenges around government funding and individual giving, foundation giving has fallen and corporations have been moving toward in-kind donations and increased focus on targeted grants. To top it off, new organizations have been popping up in response to the increasing need creating an extremely competitive market for donor dollars. The situation is severe: heightened competition, increased demand and spending, and the obvious need for more revenue. The state of the sector has transformed and the reality is that giving trends and funding resources are not going to dramatically change any time soon. What can change is how nonprofits react to this new reality.

A nonprofit can position itself for success and maximize its potential for meeting revenue goals by having a well thought out Strategic Development Plan. Prior to creating that plan, the Board and executive leadership must have insight and understanding around three key areas that have been directly impacted by our new economy:

1. Donor motivations
2. Communication strategies
3. Revenue source diversification

## Donor Motivations

Donors today are much more discerning. Their motivations and expectations of nonprofits have evolved. Understanding why donors do or do not give is vital to the success of any nonprofit.

Myriad emotions, external pressures, and internal forces drive donor generosity. Most donors give for a wide range of reasons, many of which vary from time to time, and can be difficult to identify. They can be motivated by ego, religion, ethnicity, race, pride, guilt, their peers, concern about the effect of their wealth upon future generations of heirs, or for any one, or

---

[2] "2012 State of the Nonprofit Sector survey," Nonprofit Finance Fund, April 2, 2012, http://nonprofitfinancefund.org/state-of-the-sector-surveys.
[3] Giving USA Foundation, Giving USA Report 2012.

combination of many other factors. It is a common myth and misperception that donors are motivated primarily by the tax benefits of charitable giving. In fact, when asked, donors of all sizes place this benefit near the bottom of the "motivation" scale.

Studies show that most individuals are motivated by the feeling of being able to make a difference.[4] In order of importance, the top three motivating factors for wealthy donors to give to charity are because they:

- Are moved at how the gift can make a difference
- Feel financially secure
- Believe that organization is efficient

In taking a look at the broader population, some of the reported motivations for charitable giving are:[5]

- Providing for the basic needs of the poor
- Making the community and the world a better place

Some of the common reasons individuals give to a specific organization are they:

- Believe in the mission
- Are interested in making an impact through a specific program or project
- Respect and believe in the nonprofit's work and leadership
- Trust the financial strength and efficiency

Donor motivations and behaviors will be different based on multiple demographic and psychographic factors. There are several studies that cite the differences in gender giving, giving based on income and education and even some analyze giving patterns based on geography.

As mentioned above, it is of equal value to understand why some have stopped giving. Evolving contrary beliefs, changing philanthropic priorities a dislike for certain programs or a shift in an individual's personal situation all influence the decision not to give. If a nonprofit is not providing a donor with information relevant to their individual interests and philanthropic goals it will also have a dampening impact on giving.

Detailed studies outline the four most common reasons individuals stop giving:

1. Individual or family philanthropic objectives change
2. Communication, or the lack thereof, from the nonprofit

---

[4] The 2010 Study of High Net Worth Philanthropy sponsored by Bank of America Merrill Lynch.
[5] The Center of Philosophy at Indiana University, "Understanding Donors' Motivations," October 20, 2009.

3. Solicitations from the nonprofit are overwhelming or inappropriate
4. Image or reputation of the nonprofit is tainted or negative

Major donors expect personal communication, and if they do not receive it from one nonprofit, they will seek it from others. The communication strategy for each major donor should be tailored and personal. These are the individuals from which a nonprofit is hoping to receive the greatest level of support. Leadership and staff should focus on developing relationships with these individuals and understanding their unique motivations and interests. It is important to note, however, that regardless of the deep connections and long standing relationships, donors are now, more than ever, highly sensitive and reactive to the reputation and image of the nonprofits they support.

One example of this is the 2012 Susan G. Komen Foundation debacle. In this instance, the Board of the Susan G. Komen Foundation made a decision to stop supporting Planned Parenthood. The perception of and reaction to this decision was extreme and immediate, with direct consequences on the foundation's loyal donor support. Its reputation and image were severely affected despite the almost immediate reversal of their decision. The organization suffered a significant reduction in contributions and event participation. In addition to the consequences on the revenue flow, there was significant loss in organizational leadership. Both the president and the founder felt it necessary to step down. This all happened to an organization that at the time, was the largest global charity of its kind, having fundraised in excess of $2 billion over its 30-year history. The story is a reminder of the responsibility organizational leadership, board, and staff collaboratively have for knowing the donor pool—their motivations for giving, interests in the programs and services, and the personal loyalty factors that drive their support.

## Communication Strategies

How an organization communicates with their donors and prospects is essential and the key to success no matter what the state of the economy. Frequently, communication strategies are focused on what the nonprofit wants the community to hear versus what donors and prospects want or need to know. There is very often a significant difference between the two. Additionally, in an environment where funding sources are limited, *how you ask* matters even more!

The following is an extreme example of how organizations get caught up in their needs and neglect to focus on the donor. It is all too easy for nonprofit leadership to nurture a state of panic and crisis and lose sight of having clear strategy and perspective around communication. In 2009, when the economic downturn became a reality, we would have conversations with organizations around their development and communication strategies. Here is what we heard: "We are in duress; in the middle of a crisis. We will have to cut programs and services if we don't increase our revenue through individual donations. The government is cutting our funding and it is getting more and more difficult to meet our mission goals and serve our constituency." We would ask them about their communication and development strategy. "How do you plan on engaging with donors and key prospects to realize the support you need to fulfill your mission goals?" The most common answer was, "We are going to send out a mailing or make in-person appointments to let our donors know that we are in dire straits and desperately need their support to keep our doors open and continue providing the programming to our community."

Now, as an individual reading this book, I ask you to go back in time and reflect for a moment. It's 2009 and you are wondering if you will be laid off. Your retirement portfolio is down 40 percent from where it was two years ago. You open your investment account statement and the market value has dropped once again and then you open the letter from the nonprofit you have been supporting—it's all about their crisis. At that moment, whose crisis is more important to you? Yours or the nonprofit's? I'm going to guess that the majority of you thought you and your family were the priority at that moment and you tossed the letter into the trash.

Organizations are learning, in some cases the hard way, that in order to deepen relationships with donors and realize the levels of support necessary to cover the increasing demand for programs and services, they cannot simply push a panic button. In order to successfully and effectively communicate with donors it is essential to have an understanding of donor motivations, compose a well-crafted and compelling case for support, measure programmatic impact, and develop statements to clearly communicate the benefit and effect programs and services are having both on the community and with each donor/prospect target segment.

## Revenue Source Diversification

There is so much attention spent on discussing and determining the asset allocation diversification strategies and the risks that should be considered when creating a well thought-out investment asset allocation for the endowment. Equal time and energy should be dedicated to reviewing the revenue source allocation and diversification, ensuring that an organization is not depending on one or two key sources of revenue.

As was pointed out earlier, revenue wells have dried up and funding source priorities have shifted. Since 2009, organizations depending on government funding have seen that stream diminish. Foundations have begun focusing even more on specific activities or exclusively on new and innovative programs. The result is that their money comes with more restrictions than the average individual donation. Frequently, foundations distribute one-time grants for a limited number of years, so the revenue at some point would need to be replaced to sustain a funded program. Corporate mergers have compounded the situation; corporate foundations are merging and more likely than not, the result is a reduction in total giving again affecting the nonprofits that have been the beneficiaries of those dollars. All of these factors can be limiting for many nonprofits, which is why individual donations are doubly important.

In order to balance out this shift in giving and preserve the long-term health and vitality of nonprofits, there is a need to create a balanced allocation of diversified revenue sources. Nonprofits depending too heavily on one source of funding or another have found themselves in very precarious and difficult situations. Those depending on government and corporate funds felt the most severe effects. These nonprofits were scrambling to create a plan that would make up for the gap. Nonprofits depending on individuals for a large portion of their revenue stream were in better shape. However, even they were in a position to re-evaluate and examine the opportunities they may have been leaving on the table by not having developed cultivation and stewardship plans for loyal donors. Cultivating individual donor relationships takes time and developing more sophisticated gift plans with donors is not likely to happen at the speed at which the nonprofit's need for service and revenue is growing.

Organizational leadership needs to consistently review the percentage of income coming from all sources: government, foundations, corporations, and individuals. Then, they should be drilling down even further to be sure they are maximizing the value of those relationships. It is not necessarily an equal amount of strategy and attention that should be given to each revenue source category. A significant amount of time and effort should be devoted to the individual donor. Individual contributions consistently make up the majority of the gifts given in the United States. In fact, 9 out of every 10 dollars donated here in the United States come from individuals in the form of outright gifts, bequests, and family foundation dollars. Additionally, these donations are the most likely to provide unrestricted funds to the organization, providing the nonprofit with the flexibility it needs to use the dollars where it sees the greatest need. To be successful a nonprofit will develop effective strategies to attract new donors to replace those who fall away or to increase the donor pool.

The process to ensure revenue diversifications begins with an analysis of the current revenue mix and the creation of a Strategic Development Plan. Ultimately the Strategic Development Plan will serve as the tool that outlines the communication strategy, techniques, and initiatives the organization will use to connect with prospective donors about the organizations mission and impact.

## The Strategic Development Plan

In order to understand the concept and function of the Strategic Development Plan, it is important to examine the purpose an organizational Strategic Plan. Most nonprofits go through a long and sometimes expensive process of creating and updating this three- to five-year Strategic Plan. A tremendous amount of time is typically committed. Ideas are shared and a vision and strategy for growth is identified and laid out for the organization to grow, continue to meet its mission goals, and increase its impact on the defined community. Then, a revenue gap is usually determined. The revenue gap is then translated into a goal . . . or, should we say, a GOAL. This number is usually large and generally a well-thought-out calculation of what the board and executive leadership need to balance the budget and meet growing programmatic and operational expenses. Frequently, the goals and expectations are handed to the Development department without consideration for how they will be met. The current giving environment hasn't been considered nor have donor motivations or planning behaviors. So, although the plan provides the answer to the what and where questions with vision and strategy, it does not address the how questions when it comes to the revenue goal. The document that must be created to answer the how question is the *Strategic Development Plan.*

The Strategic Development Plan defines tactical strategies and solutions for meeting the revenue goal. It provides a roadmap for the development team and a tool to create tailored development officer goals rather than creating them with broad stroke assumptions. Ultimately, the Strategic Development Plan should answer the complete question, "How will we fill the gap between our strategic vision and the revenue needed to reach it?" Since the two plans are so closely tied together, the most efficient way to develop them is to include the head of the Development department in the initial Strategic Planning discussions around goals and objectives. This is not common practice, but it is a best practice and organizations will receive a tremendous benefit from the front line perspective a development department executive will provide in the Strategic Planning discussions. Additionally, the Board will have the opportunity to obtain realistic perspective around the challenges and opportunities the development team sees in the current market environment. By involving the development executive in the strategic planning process and discussion, the Board or Strategic Planning task force or committee will create a connection between their *vision* and the reality and identify any gaps between the two.

There is a process for creating a Strategic Development Plan, just as there is for any other type of plan. It is advisable for a specific task force to be created in order to follow the process and ultimately build the plan. That task force typically includes members of the Board's Development Committee, a member of executive leadership, and the Chief Development Officer or head of Development. In order to effectively work through the process of creating this essential document, the group must:

- Understand the nonprofit's donors.
  - Analyze donor behavior, giving history, and overall fundraising culture.
  - Seek outside consultation with non-bias perspective.
  - Ask donors questions about their personal perception and motivations.
- Create effective communication tools.
  - Develop a compelling case for support.
  - Create impact statements relevant to donor interests and what they need to hear.
- Measure programmatic impact.
  - Conduct analysis of program effectiveness and efficiency.
  - Create reporting methods for donors.
- Commit to developing and reviewing the Strategic Development Plan itself.
  - Follow the suggested outline and steps.
  - Develop policies and procedures for review and reinforcement of the plan.

## Understanding Donors

Not every donor or prospective donor is going to fit into the stereotypical donor motivations depicted in the studies referenced earlier. Each nonprofit must overlay the organizational culture and dedicate time and resources to learning what is most important to them.

Additionally, donor pools grow and change. The evolution of the established donor pool can be subtle and quite sophisticated. Building and maintaining awareness around those subtleties is essential. Nonprofits are self-perpetuating organizations like any corporation or bureaucracy. Institutional thinking is the norm and every organization has certain beliefs, even myths, about itself. These evolve over the years and are presented as fact to those who come on board later. Certain assumptions which were likely true many years before persist, but often those assumptions are no longer accurate. They have a tendency to muddy reality and to implant misconceptions. Because of this and other reasons, nonprofits frequently do not understand as completely as they could the nature of those who give and why they are motivated. For this reason, it is often useful to seek outside consultation with a non-biased perspective. An experienced outsider could provide a fresh look at those who are giving and determine trends in giving patterns and unique donor motivations. The strategic development planning process provides an opportunity for a non-profit to bring together a diverse group of individuals as well. It is not uncommon for initial group discussions in the process to include volunteers, donors, community members, and prospects, along with the staff and Board members. The process is described in detail later in the chapter and provides nonprofits with an effective tool for keeping donor interests and motivations top of mind.

## Donor Pool Analysis

In addition to understanding donor motivations and donor pool trends, leadership should also understand the specific giving patterns associated with the various donor segments in its pool. It is worth the time and possible expense, if an outside consultant is retained, to analyze the greatest contributors examining patterns of loyalty and commitment. Taking such a detailed look at giving patterns and donor history gives the organizational leadership a window to explore common donor experiences, motivations, and behaviors and how specific programs, initiatives, messaging, or interaction had impact or provided inherent motivation. Examples of a few questions the task force may want to answer to conduct this valuable analysis of individual giving history are:

### The Organization Factors

- When did the individual begin donating to our organization?
- What was happening in our organization at the time?
- Who was our leader?
- What programs and services did we offer?
- Were our mission and vision different?
- How were we communicating what we were doing and how we were doing it?
- What was happening in our country/world at that time? Was it relevant to our work?

### The Individual Factors

Examine demographic and any psychographic information available. Attempt to answer questions like:

- What community does the donor live in now?
- Where did they live when they began giving?

- What was/is his or her profession?
- What was/is his or her marital status?
- Do they have children?

**The Giving Patterns**

Examine what the donors' giving patterns were and what the organization was doing that could have affected those actions. Ask questions, including:

- When did the individual begin giving?
- What was the dollar amount of the first gift?
- Has giving been consistent over the time frame?
- If there are spikes in gift amounts, what could have been the reason?
- Was the organization doing a PR or specific communication campaign?
- Was there someone with notoriety representing the organization at the time?
- What are and have been the stewardship thank you and recognition practices over time and do the giving patterns align with the attempt to build deeper relationships?

This level of detailed audit and analysis is time consuming. It is common practice for an organization to hire an outside consultant to facilitate and complete this phase of the plan. It is rare for a nonprofit to have the organizational resources available amongst the staff to spend the time and effort necessary for the outcome to be useful. Although hiring a consultant could be costly, the information obtained, even with limitations, enables an organization to be more productive in its fundraising with its existing pool and as a result realize a significant reduction in fundraising expenses. There will be insight into methods for deepening relationships and customizing gift-planning conversations. One word of caution that time and money will be wasted if a formal follow-up plan is not created. Once the investment is made in understanding this level of detail about donor pool behaviors and motivations, the Strategic Development Plan must incorporate the specific details.

It is often possible, with certain caveats, that with these analyses, nonprofit leadership can project future giving patterns and potential future revenue.

# Effective Communication Tools

The following pages discuss the effective communication tools, including how to develop case for support and impact statement documents.

# The Case for Support

The case for support is defined by the Association of Fundraising Professional's AFP Fundraising Dictionary as, *Case, n. the reasons why an organization both needs and merits philanthropic support, usually by outlining the organization's programs, current needs, and plans.* Essentially, the case for support is meant to tie donor emotion to the mission of the organization and help them to understand the importance of the cause.

The case for support should state the problem with which an organization is concerned. It should articulate, briefly, how the nonprofit is planning to solve that problem, be compelling, be persuasive, and incorporate both rational and emotional elements in its purpose. Above all the case for support should speak to the donor's heart. It must create an emotional connection and appeal to the donor's sense of generosity and philanthropic intentions.

There are myriad resources for writing a compelling case for support and the Board and staff leadership should spend time focusing on understanding the importance of a compelling case and the impact it will have on developing relationships and attracting revenue.

Here is a sampling of questions to be thinking of while developing the case for support:

- What is the problem our organization is intent on solving?
- What are our proposed or proven solutions to that problem?
- What are the resources we will use or obtain to create those solutions?
- Why do we consider our organization to be the most effective at what we do?
- What is unique about who we are serving?
- What is our goal or outcome objective?
- What is the impact we are having or plan to have on the community, the world, or society in general?
- Why should we matter to the donor?

Developing the case is a process that should ignite healthy discussion about the organization and why donors and prospects should be compelled to support it. The exercise of creating the case for support will provide the nonprofit staff, leadership, and volunteers with a tool to support their efforts in being effective community advocates.

Once completed, if compelling, the organization's case for support will articulate the cause, ignite emotion, and highlight opportunities. After the case for support statement is complete, impact statements need to be linked to each program or service of the organization to reach its mission, goals, and objectives.

## Impact Statements

An impact statement should articulate both the affect and the influence an organization's program or service is having on a community or group. As defined in the *Oxford Dictionary*, impact is a noun or verb, meaning a marked effect or influence; or having a strong effect on someone or something.

It is through the communication of impact and the development of impact statements that organizations will both retain donors and attract potential donors. Measuring programmatic impact, which we cover in the next section, and communicating the results or mission-related work to donors and prospects are essential. Donors are increasingly holding organizations accountable, not just for governance-related issues, in terms of the effectiveness of the program or service he or she is supporting.

Resources being limited and nonprofit organizations being numerous, donors have become more selective, targeted and strategic in their giving. As has been mentioned several times, donor communication should be focused on what is important to the donor, his or her interests or personal philanthropic mission to make an impact in the community. Here is a three-step process in deciding how and what to communicate in terms of organizational impact:

- *Step 1: Know what is important and relevant to the donor or prospect.* The technique: *ask.* This concept of asking an individual, foundation or corporation about what matters to them may seem second nature and simplistic. However, it seems it is so simple that it's forgotten. The majority of the organizations that we come into contact with do not have a formal process for getting to know their donors' motivations. These questions were covered in the Understanding Your Donors section of the chapter.
- *Step 2: Listen.* Once a donor or prospective donor, no matter the type—individual, foundation, or corporation—discusses or reveals why the organization is important to them and the specifics and details around that question, it is imperative that the nonprofit executive be listening or they will not be prepared for the third step.
- *Step 3: Act.* The information we collect is only as good as what we do with it, and in this case it can be very valuable to have a deep understanding of donor motivations, emotional connection, and investment interest in the organization. However, if the communication after this sharing of information and personal interaction is not customized to appeal to that individual, the value is gone.

Nonprofit professionals should consider pausing prior to asking for money and instead focus on having meaningful conversations with key loyal supporters about making an impact and fulfilling his or her philanthropic goals and finding ways to create a gift plan that is in alignment with the donor's strategy and budget. 72.6 percent of high net worth households have a strategy and philanthropic budget.[6] If an organization wants to be included in those philanthropic budgets, it will need to focus on communicating a compelling case for support, defining programmatic impact, and creating an emotional connection with donors and prospects.

## Measuring Programmatic Impact

The discerning nature of donors has been mentioned several times. Information gathering for the purpose of satisfying selective giving and rising expectations is the norm.

There has always been an acute awareness of nonprofit expense ratios. Deeming an organization efficient meant they kept their costs low and the visibility of their mission high. However, donors' expectations reach beyond simply measuring expense ratios. When measuring programmatic impact, organizations are answering the question, "How is this program effective?" Donors today are looking to make an impact. They want to see results. In fact, when we look at the younger generation of philanthropists, their giving behaviors exhibit the clear expectation that when making a philanthropic investment, they will see results in order to confirm that it was the right choice for their gifting dollars. Then they may consider investing in that organization in the future.

In order to measure programmatic impact and provide donors with these results, many nonprofit organizations need to implement change. When discussing a major gift for programmatic support, the development officer must be able to explain why that program is effective and how they will measure results. It is no longer acceptable to respond with "this is the way we have always implemented our programs." What this means for most organizations is that they will need to develop a process for measuring effectiveness, efficiencies, and overall impact of their programs prior to asking for donor support. Each program or initiative will have a separate and unique set of measurement factors. Measuring programmatic impact is a detailed process and can be time consuming. Once a detailed description of the program initiative has been determined, the questions the organization needs to answer are straightforward.

---

[6] The 2010 Study of High Net Worth Philanthropy sponsored by Bank of America Merrill Lynch.

Some of the most general and typically applicable questions a programmatic impact measurement report would need to answer are as follows:

- What need does the program fill?
- How does filling that need help the organization reach its mission goals?
- What activities took place? Were the activities that actually took place in the initial plan? If not, what was different from the plan and why?
- What was the total cost of the project and what is the detailed breakout of those expenses? How did those expenses compare to the originally budgeted expenses?
- What were the results and specific details around the impact-related outcomes? Did the program meet the measurable objectives that were set initially? What other objectives or outcomes resulted from the program—perhaps unplanned positive outcomes?
- What were the learning experiences from this project?
- How will the organization take what it learned and use the information and/or progress to springboard it into the next initiative?

The exercise of measuring programmatic impact will not only serve to provide donors with the information they need to make decisions about current and future gifts, it will provide the organizational leadership with the details and information needed to analyze whether or not they are running the organization efficiently. What is more critical as a nonprofit leader or fiduciary than knowing if the programs and services you are providing are effectively meeting mission goals and being run in a cost-effective and efficient manner? The programmatic impact analysis will provides valuable information that should be considered when developing the Strategic Development Plan.

## The Strategic Development Planning Process

Optimally, the Strategic Development Planning process should happen through a collaborative effort between executive leadership, members of the Board (Development Committee), and the head of the Development department, and we suggest including representation from the organization's volunteers, donors, and prospects for initial conversations and brainstorming. The group can come together with the charge to analyze, review and identify opportunities for creating the plan. This gets us to breaking down the steps in the process.

The steps in the process include:

## Analyzing the Current Situation

- Discuss the case for support. Is it compelling?
- Review the Strengths, Weaknesses, Opportunities, and Threats (SWOT) analysis (usually detailed in the Strategic Plan).
- Determine if the review sources are diversified.
  - Do they make sense for the organization's long-term goal?
  - Is there something that is obviously missing or over-weighted?
- Evaluate current fundraising methods.
  - What are the costs associated with each?
  - What is the mission impact associated with each?
  - Which are the most cost efficient?
- Discuss staff and volunteer resources.

## Identifying the Opportunities

- Discuss potential donors/prospects and new target segments.
- Define how the nonprofit and its programs and services are perceived in the community.
- Review the impact the programs and services are having on the community at large. Also review for a specific group of individuals.
- Identify priorities for new or enhanced fundraising activities.
- Discuss what additional investment or resources may be needed to implement the plan.
- Set realistic goals; keep the plan timelines and budget realistic.
- Create the plan.

## The Plan

The end result should be a clear, concise, and functional document that will provide the organization with a roadmap through the process of implementing initiatives and measuring results. The final document should:

- Identify the goals and objectives of the development team.
- Outline priorities.
- Articulate a compelling case for support and impact goals.
- Provide a tactical, prioritized fundraising plan.
- Identify and classify target segments of donors or prospects.
- Describe initiatives—strategies, tactics, events, and activities.
- Define timelines and resource allocations.
- Include measurable outcomes.

The process of developing a Strategic Development Plan will result in more than just a final planning document. The sharing of perspective by volunteers, staff, donors, and board members will provide valuable insight to the nonprofit leadership team.

It is common for nonprofit organizations to do the same thing they have always done in terms of development initiatives like events and mailings. It is not necessarily common practice to evaluate the return on investment of those initiatives in terms of mission impact and overall effectiveness. The Strategic Development Plan will provide structure to each development initiative. It will identify the target segments, activities, and initiatives planned to reach those segments, budget, timeline, and responsibility associated with each. These elements laid out in a formal plan will enable the leadership team with measurement tools to evaluate results versus the plan. It will help provide structure around the conversations associated with the questions:

- How are we doing in our development efforts?
- What is working?
- What isn't working?
- What do we want to do again?

Often outreach and communication with target donors and prospects needs to be fine-tuned and tweaked on a regular basis, taking into consideration the economy, evolution of the donors, and growth and change in the organization. Having the plan in place will help keep the need at top of mind because once a plan exists regular review will drive the conversations.


## The Importance of Planned Giving As a Strategic Development Tool: Building Endowment with Planned Gifts

Planned gifts are one source of revenue that a nonprofit had to have been committed to cultivating prior to the Great Recession in order to potentially benefit from the gifts during the economic downturn. However, as was alluded to earlier in the chapter, many nonprofits continue to work assiduously just to survive this difficult period and are losing sight of their long-term well-being and health of the endowment by concentrating almost all of their energy on insuring the operations are strong during the near term.

The prospect of generational wealth transfer is very optimistic. Every nonprofit has the opportunity to capitalize on the new assets being added into the financial stream of philanthropic dollars within the next decade and beyond, as one generation transfers its wealth (however reduced it is from market forces) to their children, to nonprofits, and to government in the form of taxes. Many of these donors were entrepreneurs, built their businesses years ago, and are the same type of hard-working, business-owning, understated, affluent family that was portrayed so vividly in the book *Millionaire Next Door: The Surprising Secrets of America's Wealthy* by Thomas J. Stanley and William D. Danko (Gallery Books, 1998).

The majority of millionaires in the United States are not hedge fund managers or Internet moguls—they are small business people with the bulk of their wealth hidden from view, living in nice but unassuming homes and driving Fords and Cadillacs, not BMWs and Mercedes-Benzes. They have accumulated assets in their businesses and conservative investments. These are individuals who may or may not have gone to college. Many will leave funds to nonprofits for a variety of reasons we will review. Simply put, a nonprofit organization must capitalize on the opportunity to cultivate the current entrepreneurial generation, as it may be many years until our country experiences the next wave of wealth accumulation.

## What Is Planned Giving?

Planned giving, sometimes referred to as gift planning, may be defined as a method of supporting non-profits and charities that enables philanthropic individuals or donors to make larger gifts than they could make from their incomes. While some planned gifts provide a life-long income to the donor, others use estate and tax planning techniques to provide for charity and other heirs in ways that maximize the gift and/or minimize its impact on the donor's estate. Thus, by definition, a planned gift is any major gift, made in lifetime or at death, as part of a donor's overall financial and/or estate planning.[7] Planned gifts can be very complex or very simple. Some can offer significant donor tax advantages today for assets that don't actually transfer to the charity until a later date. Planned giving vehicles include charitable vehicles such as bequests made through a will, charitable gift annuities, life insurance and IRA beneficiary designations, charitable remainder trusts, and charitable lead trusts to name a few.

There are myriad resources for beginners to learn more specifically the mechanics of the various planned giving vehicles available, including excellent online resources like the Planned Giving Design Center (www.pgdc.com) or resources like the Partnership for Philanthropic Planning (PPP). PPP holds annual conferences on planned giving topics (www.pppnet.org). This group also offers regional planned giving council meetings around the country providing timely educational topics and trainings.

---

[7] "What Is Planned Giving?" PlannedGiving.com, www.plannedgiving.com.

## Why Is Planned Giving Strategically Relevant?

By incorporating planned giving as a development tool in conversations with donors, a nonprofit will be able to:

- Open up all of the opportunities to capture a portion of this wealth transfer.
- Provide the nonprofit with further diversification of its revenue sources.
- Build a pipeline of funding for the future of the organization.
- Provide donors with more gift planning options.
- Build endowment.

While there has been much discussion about the transfer of wealth and the implications it has for the nonprofit community, not every nonprofit organization is in a position to benefit. An organization must design a plan to seize opportunities to receive this money.

Additionally, in order to successfully implement this plan, an organization must have fundraising professionals who are not solely focused on meeting their annual goals, but truly engaged with donors around long-term strategies that could be beneficial to the donor as well as to the nonprofit.

# Donor Values That Affect Their Legacy Giving

The biggest motivation for a donor to make a significant gift to a select charity in the form of a planned gift is because they believe that organization is the singularly most effective instrument to achieve a charitable objective. All other issues are secondary—they have to believe passionately that the organization is the best at what it does. That means that the reputation of the organization is paramount to preserving the loyalty of donors.

Are there other values of a donor that affect his or her inclination to be charitable through legacy gifts that an organization needs to be aware of to cultivate potential donors? Of course! Affluent individuals want to prevent their children from having unproductive lives, the sense of immortality has been a motivating factor for centuries, and then there are those who are motivated by moral or religious obligations.

More than a decade ago, Warren Buffett, appearing in a news broadcast, said in effect, "I want to give my children enough so that they do something, but not so much that they do nothing."[8] What Buffett was referring to was

---

[8] Richard I. Kirkland Jr. and Carrie Gottlieb, "Should You Leave It All to the Children?" CNN Money, September 29, 1986.

that many families, not just those worth billions, have a great concern about the effect of their wealth upon the well-being of their heirs.

Many families of affluence worry that their children will become afflicted with what has been termed by anti-consumer author John de Graaf as *affluenza*,[9] defined by him as a *"painful, contagious, socially transmitted condition of overload, debt, anxiety, and waste resulting from the dogged pursuit of more."* In the many years since the term was coined, affluenza has also come to mean, especially when referring to the second generation of an affluent family, *as spoiled, feeling entitled, and expecting material wealth without personal economic or socially redeeming productivity.*

As they plan their estates, many affluent families are drawing conclusions similar to those of Warren Buffett that leaving too much money to children or grandchildren could have a corrosive, corrupting influence on them that could diminish their personal drive to become productive citizens.

Donors have been motivated for generations by having their names associated with a charity so that they could reach some form of immortality. In 1929, archeologists uncovered a mosaic floor of a 1,500-year-old synagogue in Beit Alpha in northern Israel that had inlaid a dedication to a father and son who paid for and completed the mosaic.

This sense of immortality, the sense of making a lasting difference, can provide tremendous satisfaction to someone who has reached his or her top level of material success. It is a sensation that only a nonprofit can bestow upon an affluent individual. It provides a sense of spiritual contentment that comes from knowing a gift will help individuals in perpetuity. It helps answer for many individuals the questions, why am I here, what has my life meant, and what can I do to be remembered well by my family and the generations who follow me?

Others are motivated by a sense of moral or religious obligation to give back to others. Many of the millionaires next door who built their businesses in their towns have a sense of paying back to their communities for the success they were able to build there.

A major challenge for a nonprofit is to glean from its major donors what their values are, and to determine how those values can be memorialized through a legacy gift to the organization. The opportunity associated with overcoming that challenge is deep and meaningful relationships with loyal donors and a pipeline of future funding through legacy gifts.

---

[9] John de Graaf, David Wann, and Thomas H. Naylor, *Affluenza: The All-Consuming Epidemic* (San Francisco: Berrett-Kohler Publishers, 2001).

## End of Chapter Review Questions

Here are some questions you should consider and answer after reading this chapter:

- Do you know what motivates your donors?
- Are your programs consistently in alignment with your mission?
- Do you have an organized, consistent communication strategy?
- Is your communication and marketing donor centered?
- Are you telling them what you want them to know or what they want to hear?
- Is your case for support compelling?
- Can staff and volunteer leadership articulate the impact you are having?
- Are your revenue sources diversified?
- Is the development plan for the organization formally written and strategic?
- Are your development teams and board members working collaboratively to uncover and discover opportunities?
- What is your process? Do you have a Strategic Development Plan? Is it connected to the organization's Strategic Plan?

## Summary

The nonprofit organization that implements a formal strategic development planning process truly thinks about the audience in their donor and prospect communication and creates initiatives to broaden their reach and engage with a diversified group of revenue sources, will possess awareness and efficiency that will place it above the rest. It will be in a better position to fulfill the rising demand for services and overcome revenue challenges. If it incorporates planned giving into the development mix, it will be further diversifying revenue, capturing a portion of the wealth transfer to come, providing long-term planning solutions both to fill the donors' needs and the future stability of the endowment.

Despite the pain caused by the Great Recession, nonprofits continue to have tremendous opportunities by engaging in cultivating donors who have given consistently to them. Using the right development representative, they need to engage in discussions with each prospective endowment donor to understand the donor's passions and interests. They need to ascertain which of the various planned giving strategies would be most helpful to the donor and educate them about those strategies. If necessary, they must meet with the donor and their professionals to craft a set of planned giving strategies that will work well for the donor, their family, and the charity.

No matter how complete the process of creating a development strategy, the end result will not be effective without a clear understanding of the donor pool and today's donor, what is referred to here as the modern donor. The next chapter takes a deep look into evolving donor expectations, donor pool characteristics, and some strategy associated with increasing donor pools.

# CHAPTER 13

# The Evolution of Donors—Trends and Truths

## *Fundraising Is the Lifeblood of Any Charity*

Raising enough money is the single greatest challenge nonprofit organizations face each day. Keeping an organization's lights on so that it can fulfill its mission is the constant preoccupation of most nonprofit Boards and staff. The situation is especially acute at the highest levels when it comes to unrestricted contributions, for although the most loyal donors may understand the need to support an organization's operating expense, there is an increasing tendency for donors to specify the use to which their contribution is to be put. Obtaining annual general operating funds can be daunting.

So, who is giving and how? It is imperative that nonprofit leadership understands today's donor and the evolving donor pool. What are the key factors, and how are donors choosing to give? Raising money in this new environment is dependent on understanding the shift in the way donors think and act. We will refer to this new generation of donor as "the modern donor." The modern donor tends to give larger donations to a small number of nonprofits, rather than smaller amounts to a larger number. They want to make a measurable impact and be pivotal to the success of a project.

## The Modern Donor

Understanding the modern donor is a vital part of future planning for any nonprofit. These individuals have been the subject of extensive research, and it is well documented that they want to make a difference, to give back some of what they earned or inherited. Myriad studies have shown that they have a number of shared goals, most of which come from their own entrepreneurial experience or are logical extensions of it. They understand the value of giving as part of a group so they can leverage financial resources. They understand the long-standing traditions of American philanthropy and they are willing to learn from others' successes as well as failures in their decision-making. In many ways, they are not all that different from the traditional donor. The modern donor, however, is also asking for something few nonprofits are able to provide: Concrete proof that contributions make a difference in their mission. A portion of this demand comes from the modern donor's own experience in business. They've invested large sums and learned from experience to insist on seeing a genuine impact from the investment. They are experienced in measuring results, seeing the effectiveness of a marketing campaign, and evaluating growth, sales, or various product strategies. They have learned how to devise a strategy that can be measured in its impact. Investing resources, measuring change, and then determining if the goal has been achieved are skills they have finely honed in achieving business success. This is all familiar territory and it seems to them quite logical to extend it to the world of nonprofits. And they are right to do so.

One of the reasons why the modern donor feels comfortable demanding proof of impact is the incredible array of charities to give to, the crude analogy being that they can charity shop for the nonprofit that will agree to provide them metrics to measure the impact of their charitable giving.

In addition to the increased number of nonprofits, donors have a wide range of gifting options available to them. There are now myriad creative giving vehicles that can be employed, each offering its own distinct advantages. This increase in options and flexibility creates another hurdle for nonprofits to jump when trying to engage with donors and gain support. When it comes to contributing, the modern donor may give directly to an established nonprofit, or he or she might create their own vehicle through which they funnel their charitable contributions like their own donor advised fund or private foundation.

## Donor Advised Fund

A donor advised fund (DAF) is a charitable giving vehicle held and managed by a public charity. It provides individuals or families with a flexible, low cost grant-making solution. Unlike a private foundation, there is no minimum distribution requirement for a DAF and most DAF products are turnkey solutions. A DAF also provides donors with an alternative to making a major gift directly to the nonprofit. They will receive their charitable deduction at the time the gift is made to the Donor Advised Fund and they have flexibility around when the funds will be granted. A growing number of donors, individuals, and families have created these vehicles.

Many charities receive an increasing number of gifts from donor advised funds run by community foundations, other charities, or by financial services firms. A charity considering establishing its own DAF program should strongly consider the costs of building an infrastructure to create such a program, and the efficacy of doing so, since it is likely that distributions will be made to a spectrum of other charities unless the initial operational agreements put guardrails on the donor's choices for charitable distributions. If the restrictions are too prohibitive for a donor, they can decide to create a DAF through another program and entity.

## Private Foundation

A private foundation is a nonprofit entity set up by an individual, a family, or a business to serve a philanthropic purpose. This charitable tool fosters family involvement and provides control and flexibility over the assets and the giving.

Private foundations have become very popular charitable vehicles with modern donors, those individuals and families who like to be in control of all grants and investments. It can be a great vehicle to engage multiple generations of the same family, and it can last in perpetuity, just like a DAF.

It is common for the modern donor to use several such vehicles; that is, to have, in effect, a balanced portfolio of giving, just as they have for their investments. These vehicles provide them with the same personal tax benefits while allowing them the time and flexibility they need to be selective about the nonprofits they would like to invest in. Nonprofit leadership and development teams need to understand the mentality and characteristics of the donor and develop communication and cultivation strategies that will appeal to them.

## Characteristics of the Modern Donor

There are several characteristics that are typical of the modern donors, as they:

- Do not take advice from traditional nonprofit sources like development directors and advancement professionals.
- Rely on peers in making decisions and are more likely to seek out such a peer who is already active in philanthropy.
- Learn how to deal with this new world from their workplace experience and entrepreneurial instincts.
- Believe in the power of networking.
- Place great reliance on technology.
- Require results and tangible impact in exchange for their investment.
- Expect organizational efficiency and will seek information to support the proof of the organization's sound policies and prudent practices.

## Connecting with the Modern Donor

Connecting with this donor is very different from connecting with the traditional donor. Keeping in mind characteristics of the modern donor, there are specific techniques that will enable an organization to more effectively reach these individuals.

- Connect with individuals through their social or business network
- Engage in meaningful conversations with loyal volunteers
- Share examples and facts around the direct impact the organization is having
- Create a diversified communication plan that includes social media outreach and a comprehensive, dynamic website that is easy to navigate.
- Engage with key qualified prospects around interest in volunteering and becoming more involved in the organizational leadership.
- Leverage Board members' peer groups and spheres of influence

Establish metrics and set up individual meetings with the most likely prospects to give your nonprofit greater credibility and to get them to think of your charity as a conduit to carry forward their philanthropic ideas.

An organization must employ new methods for identifying and bringing the modern, generational donor into its donor pool. It may mean forming an institutional connection with his or her foundation or organization and leveraging new technology. It takes time and resources, but it is well worth the effort.

## Transformations in Giving Patterns

In this post-Great Recession period, giving patterns have been affected by myriad factors such as:

- Giving proclivities of foreign-born donors
- Gender
- Ethnicity
- Age

There are studies revealing the evolving nature of charitable giving based on all of these factors and keeping up with the nuances can be a job in itself. The key to success will be for development teams and organizational leadership to capitalize on the information revealed through the studies and, from those descriptive trends and valuable insights, to develop techniques focused on engaging with donors and next generation of philanthropists.

At its core, fundraising consists of asking people to give to support a certain cause. This is the case whether approaching an individual, corporation, or foundation. Many organizations have the tendency to approach a foundation or corporation as a business. The reality is that no matter what form the prospect is in, individual donor, foundation, or corporation, they are all made up of individual decision makers. Nonprofits need to keep in mind that they are always dealing directly with people. It is essential to motivate and exert influence over those capable of giving, or those who are in control of the giving decision process. Donor motivations were addressed during the Strategic Development planning chapter. Addressed here is the broader picture and key factors affecting giving patterns and donor pools.

## Giving Proclivities of Foreign-Born Donors

One of the factors that will affect the giving patterns of the donor pool is the relevance and diminishing importance of an organization's mission to the younger generations. Consider the example of a charity with a mission to help the population in the foreign country where the bulk of its donors hail from. Those who immigrated to the United States still have relatives in their land of birth and as their economic circumstances here improve, they give to the charity. Over the years, many of them begin to do quite well financially and they give even more. In time, their adult children give. But eventually the connection to the old country becomes distant as the family moves into its third and fourth generations. All the while those who immigrated are deceased and are not being replaced by significant numbers of new immigrants. Contributions dwindle. This is the life cycle of many nonprofits' donor pools.

The process of creating the Strategic Development Plan should reveal this factor as a key issue when the organization is developing strategy around future revenue potential. Strategies should be developed to leverage the loyal donor relationships and capitalize on some of the opportunities of how this factor affects the evolving donor pool. An organization may want to consider developing a Heritage Preservation Initiative to create connections and bridges between the younger and older generations around heritage preservation through communication strategies, programs, and events. The objective is to exhibit the impact the organization has had on heritage for that younger generation and reinforce the point by involving the older generations.

## Ethnicity

The ethnic makeup of America is changing. That has always been the case and will continue to be for the foreseeable future. Twenty-five percent of the American population today is composed of those with either Hispanic or

African-American ancestry. The percentage of Hispanics is projected to increase and in the immediate decades the proportion of the population of Asian ancestry will also increase significantly.

These growing statistics introduce a whole new issue and subject worthy of mastery by development professionals around the culture of giving. Many immigrants come to America from countries where there is no history of philanthropy. Some foreign governments fund programs operated by charities; in other countries, it is the church that primarily takes care of the poor. The concept of charitable giving can be very new to some immigrant populations. Finding a way to reach emerging foreign-born communities, to educate them, and pull them into your pool has never been more important.

An organization will want to be sure that it has its finger on the pulse of the changing ethnic makeup in its community. Additionally, development and communication teams must understand the philanthropic values for the dominating ethnic culture. And finally, communication strategies and cultivation plans should focus on two key messages: one message around the value the organization brings to the community and a second message clearly stating the fact that the organization depends on private donations from individuals.

The implications for nonprofits of the evolving and ever-changing American population should be self-evident. Nonprofits must develop ways to approach the non-traditional groups that are forming an ever-greater part of our society. An organization should think about how their programs and services fill the evolving needs in the community, it should find ways to relate to the philanthropic culture and ethics of the group, and optimally the leadership team and staff need to reflect the diversity in the community and donor pool.

## Gender

We know the American population is getting older, and richer, but it is *who* is getting older, living longer, and becoming much richer that is having a profound effect on the nature of American wealth and philanthropy. Not only are trillions of dollars about to change generational hands, but the greater percentage of those who will come into this wealth will be women. Statistically, women live longer than men. More women today handle their own investments and finances. Women are taking control of family businesses and managing family foundations. Women with ever-growing financial power are poised to, or have already, become the dominant force in and for American nonprofits.

By the year 2030, 54 percent of American Baby Boomers will be women. Most importantly, studies show that this growing group of women is statistically more charitable then men. Baby Boomer and older women give 89 percent more to charity than men.[1] Additionally, in households in the top 25 percent of permanent income, Baby Boomer and older women give 156 percent more to charity than men.[2] Nonprofit organizations need to understand the behaviors and motivations unique to women and they should also be proactively developing communications, programs, and strategies to appeal to this fast growing group of philanthropists.

Studies are showing women's motivations and behaviors around charitable giving to be unique. According to the summary findings in The 2011 Study of High Net Worth Women's Philanthropy sponsored by Bank of America Merrill Lynch:

- Women spend more time than men on due diligence before making decisions about giving to a charitable organization.
- Women expect a deeper level of communication with the organizations they support and place greater importance than men on the efficiency and effectiveness of the organization and hearing about the impact of their gift.
- Women want to be actively involved with an organization and its mission, with volunteering being among the most important motivations for women to give.
- Women are more likely than men to stop giving to an organization they had previously supported whereas men tend to support the same causes year after year.

There is no question that women are a powerful force in philanthropy and nonprofit organizations that understand women's motivations have fostered opportunities to leverage their needs. Some examples of these are women giving circles, women-focused events, or educational programs directly addressing women's concerns. No matter what the venue, program, or cultivation strategy, the focus and objective when engaging with women should be to educate, engage, ignite passion, and show results.

Women want to be involved and they want a hand in making the world a better place. They want to be active in finding solutions for global issues. They are passionate and resourceful. This is true not only of the Baby Boomer generation, but even of the Gen Xers (those born between 1961 and 1980). This leads us to the generational factor and the differences in philanthropy among different generations.

---

[1] Women's Philanthropy Institute, "Women Give 2012: New Research about Women and Giving," August 2012.
[2] Ibid.

## Age

America's increasing average age will also have a profound impact upon charitable giving. The fastest growing segment of our population are those 85 years of age and older. In fact, there are approximately 100,000 Americans who are older than 100 years, so to gain access to this increasing percentage of the population, nonprofits must act now.

Aging seniors have concerns about outliving their wealth. The result might be a lowered or static commitment to annual charitable giving as they retain funds to provide for their needs. For this reason, it may very well be that this group of aging seniors will be more receptive to charitable giving through bequests and charitable estate planning tools like charitable trusts. Nonprofit organizations need to be proactive about developing planned giving programs to cultivate the older loyal donors in their donor pools. It is essential for them to always keep in mind that the gift planning is about designing the right gift to meet the donor's needs and that includes personal financial and tax needs in addition to the individuals' need to make an impact or leave a legacy through that organization.

In addition to the challenges and opportunities associated with our aging population and the growing numbers and influence of the baby boomer generation, we also must recognize distinct culture and specific giving habits our Generation X and Y donors exemplify. As a group they tend to hold less loyalty to specific causes and institutions than their parents and grandparents. They are also inclined to be less trusting, expect greater accountability, and require more detailed information. They tend to be less long term in their expectations and want to give where they can see the money create a measurable change.

Gen X and Y donors want to see immediate results. They are the generation of instant gratification. Their thoughts around nonprofit involvement are that their time and connections are a gift and they will invest in the organization, but they want to see results in order to consider re-investing. Nonprofits don't typically believe they need to prove themselves. Historically, the work the organizations did—helping people or animals, saving lives, feeding the poor—was enough. This new expectation is a huge philosophical and cultural shift. Leadership should be tuned into this shift and focus on how they will begin reporting return on investment (ROI) to donors.

Nonprofits must change not just the type of information they share with the new generation of donor, but how they share it is also key. Direct mail is not the most effective communication tool for Gen X and Y donors. Nonprofit communication teams need to be on top of evolving technology and be sure the organization has a presence on myriad sites and electronic venues to build awareness with this generation. Studies show that younger generations are counting on a variety of information sources. Similar to the baby boomers, they look to their peers and mainstream media for information and opportunities initially. Websites and e-mail communications are ranked as most important and the Convio March 2010 study points out that, "Facebook and other social media register as somewhat significant charity information channels for Gen X and Y."[3]

Although this group of donors may not represent the vital prospect target segment for major gifts or significant capital campaign or eminent legacy gifts, building relationships and loyalty with this generation is essential. Studies show the group to be philanthropic, however they are not, at this point, showing signs of loyalty to a particular organization. They are persuaded and motivated by their peers, the media, and random opportunities to support the current issues around the world. A nonprofit should focus development strategies for this target segment on building loyalty and involving the group in organization. Some ideas to consider would be cultivating a Junior Board and engaging the younger generation as future leaders for the organization; engaging a group of volunteers in brainstorming program implementation, and involving a diverse age group of donors and prospects in the strategic development planning process.

There are myriad strategies and ideas that can be implemented to address all of the factors involved in changing donor demographics. The key is for nonprofit leadership and development teams to be aware of the shift and proactively create strategies to create and capitalize on opportunities rather than waiting until it's too late and revenue wells have dried up.

## Growing the Donor Pool

Every nonprofit organization has a certain number of people who are aware of its cause and a certain number of them who are willing to give. But because of those who drop out or pass on, an organization must continue to funnel new people into its donor pool. There are many development techniques and strategies for growing the pool. There are myriad books, seminars, and papers written about the various methods of fundraising, the costs and effectiveness of each type and there are several renditions of the classic fundraising pyramid showing one-time or event giving at the base, annual giving, major giving, and at the very top planned/deferred gifts. Any development executive will have a thorough understanding of each of these fundraising areas and will incorporate a balance of each into the Strategic Development Plan. This book is not meant to outline fundraising

---

[3] Vinay Bhagat, Pam Loeb, and Mark Rovner, "The Next Generation of American Giving," Convio, March 2010, www.convio.com/files/next-gen-whitepaper.pdf.

fundamentals, but rather provide a few key strategies and ideas that organizational leadership can implement to leverage what we know about the Modern Donor and what we are learning about the characteristics of the evolving donor pool in this post-Great Recessionary period.

With that in mind, this section will outline three key suggested strategies:

1. Leverage loyal donor relationships to connect with their circle of friends and peer groups.
2. Engage in development cultivation dialogue with volunteers.
3. Engage the Board in the development process.

## Leverage Loyal Donor Relationships

Studies have shown that high net worth individuals depend on their peers for information and advice when it comes to their philanthropic planning. There is great value in having a loyal major donor make introductions to their friends and associated affiliations like corporations, foundations, and professional groups. The organization's loyal contributors may or may not be aware of the value they could provide and need they could be filling by facilitating introductions. Executive leadership, Board members, and the development executive should work together to:

- Identify a targeted number of key major donors.
- Conduct a one-on-one meeting with each to discuss their role in helping the organization grow its donor pool.
- Determine the comfort level and willingness of each individual to make introductions.
- Design a strategy for facilitating those introductions—intimate home party or introduction to an association group like a fraternity or sorority or a club such as Rotary. Or, perhaps a corporate introduction is more appropriate.

Whatever the strategy, the donor should feel comfortable sharing with the group his or her passion for and commitment to the nonprofit's mission. The nonprofit leadership team should focus on developing relationships during this introductory moment, whether it is an intimate cocktail reception or a group presentation. The key to turning any of these peer introductions into new donor relationships is the development and implementation of a cultivation plan. The donor has opened the door for the organizational leadership to have a conversation with a new prospective donor. At this point, it is up to the organizational leadership to seize the opportunity, uncover potential interest, and develop relationships.

## Engage in Development Cultivation Dialogue with Volunteers

Volunteers are sometimes overlooked as an important strategic target segment during the strategic development planning process. Many times nonprofit organizations are focused on volunteer management in the sense that
they need to manage the resources available through the volunteer base in
order to expand organizational capacity. However, it is essential not to lose
sight of the opportunity.

Volunteers are already making an investment in the organization. Some
may be donors, but all are investing their time. This group is typically very
passionate and knowledgeable about the organization's work, and its
mission, programs, and services. Some may have a direct connection
with the benefactors of the mission-based programs and services. In
other words, they personally see and feel the impact the organization is
having. Others, like Board members, may be extremely involved with the
strategic direction and operations of the organization. In any case, it is
essential for the leadership team and staff to focus on getting to know the
volunteers on a more personal level. To understand *who* they are and
why the organization is important to them. The process is simple. It begins
with taking the time to develop the relationships and ask important
questions, like:

- Why did you decide to volunteer for this organization?
- Do you have a personal connection to the mission and impact?
- Is your motivation professional development?
- What is most important to you about what we do?
- What is the value you feel you bring to the organization in your role as a
  volunteer?
- Do you feel we are making an impact on our community?
- Do you feel like you make an impact in your role? Is it the impact you had
  hoped to make when you began volunteering?
- Are you involved with other organizations?
- What do you do with them?
- What motivates you to keep you involved as an active volunteer?

The answers to these questions are relevant no matter what level the
volunteer in the organization. Whether the individual is volunteering on the
Board, a task force, in the thrift shop, or giving tours of the campus or
grounds, they are an active part of the organizational culture and a key
target segment for growing the prospect base and eventually the donor
pool. As was pointed out earlier, individuals are motivated by emotion
and believing that they can make a difference through their donations.
Since volunteers are already involved and making a personal investment

in the organization, development staff, and leadership need to spend the time finding out why. Cultivating the volunteer's interest and eventually presenting gift planning opportunities can facilitate that volunteer in making the lasting impact on the organization through a charitable gift.

Not all volunteers are going to be major or legacy gift prospects, but no matter their personal capacity to give, there is an incredible advantage to getting to know them better. It will provide insight and understanding around who is passionate about the mission and what is the perceived impact the organization is having. Additionally, volunteers provide perspective as eyes and ears in the community. Organizations can leverage this valuable insight by involving volunteers in the strategic development planning process. Investing time and energy into volunteer cultivation can present new gift planning opportunities and offer very valuable insight into community perspective and potential opportunities to help grow the donor pool.

Finally, although the focus in this section has been on the process of building the relationships with volunteers, it would be an oversight not to mention that, when polled about their volunteer hours, recent studies[4] show number of volunteer hours high net worth households spend with an organization directly correlates with the dollar amount of their donations. The greater the quantity of hours volunteered, the larger the donation.

## Engage the Board in the Development Process

In addition to being dedicated volunteers, Board members are an organization's key advocates. There are typically two main goals of the development team in working with the Board. The first is to engage with each Board member as a donor. The second is to empower each Board member to be an effective community advocate.

Although some organizations may have full Board support and participation in their fundraising campaigns, many do not. Often the difference between an organization that has Board participation in the fundraising efforts and one that does not is the grassroots culture of the organization. If a Board is formed by the founder of the organization and brought together to support the effort to advance a mission by contributing advice and expertise to run the organization, there may be no expectations set around personal financial contributions. Even after the organization has evolved and is

---

[4] The 2010 Study of High Net Worth Philanthropy sponsored by Bank of America Merrill Lynch.

perhaps in the mature stage of the organizational lifecycle, the Board may be more focused on their personal fiduciary responsibilities and organizational transparency, both such prominent issues concerning nonprofits today.

However, all this being true and relevant, the Board members' commitment to the development efforts of the organization and his/her own personal financial commitment are of equal importance to all of the other responsibilities a Board member takes on. The leadership team and development executive must take an active role in fostering the development efforts and participation of the Board. Board members are volunteers with a very important role in helping advance and preserve the mission of the organization. It is up to the Executive Director and the development team to understand *why* each of the individuals serving on the Board has made such a significant commitment and dedicated time and energy to the cause. Time and effort should go into developing a relationship with each Board member, understanding his or her emotional connection to the organization, his or her capacity to give, and then support should be provided to help him or her design the right gift.

In addition to knowing the answers to the questions in the previous section on volunteers, it is also important for the Executive Director and the development team to understand what goals each Board member has and the impact they are hoping to have during their term as a board member or on a specific committee. Here are some additional questions to consider in order to understand and deepen relationships with Board members:

- What questions do you have regarding specifically what is happening with our donors, programs, or development challenges and opportunities that may not have had the opportunity to discuss in Board or committee meetings?
- Are you comfortable articulating our case for support? The impact statements?
- Do you have a personal passion statement to share with friends, colleagues, and peers in the community that articulates the purpose of the dedication, time, and commitment you have made here?
- Do you have a vision of the impact you would like to make around our mission as an individual or collectively as a Board?
- Where do you think we will have the biggest impact?
- What is most exciting about our Strategic Plan and the direction it will take us in?
- What is your vision and hope of where we will be in three years?

In addition to the Executive Director and the development team spending the time to get to know each Board member personally, it is important for the organization to have set expectations around Board member participation in events, activities, and personal giving. Having a Development Committee of the Board to support this effort is a helpful best practice. This committee can develop some of the policies discussed later in the book and they can be the champions for creating a culture of development support on the Board.

The Development Committee would also be able to provide some perspective during discussions around the roles and responsibilities of the Board members in the development process, including minimum gift commitments or other financial support guidelines. It is important to have a peer group discussion about how gift commitment expectations should be designed for Board members because each member brings unique value and an organization would not want to discourage talented and important contributors based solely on giving capacity. A policy should be developed to establish the Board's roles and responsibilities and those should include gift expectations. One of the tools the Development Committee could help to create is a *Menu of Opportunities*, a tool that can be created to help guide Development staff conversations with individual Board members around their personal contribution, participation in the events and activities for the year, and identify his or her commitment to be involved in development strategies. Such a tool sets expectations and creates clarity for the Board member's role in development and associated activities throughout the year. Ideally these policies and practices are set in the beginning stages of the nonprofit lifecycle and they are inherently part of the organizational culture.

Having 100 percent Board giving is in itself helpful as a factor for growing the donor pool. However, the ripple effect of those gifts will have an even greater affect. It is a very strong statement for an organization to be able to say they have full support—100 percent Board participation and charitable gift support. The message to the community is clearly that the individuals who are most involved and dedicated to the efficient operations, strategy, and vision for the future of the organization are confidently invested in its future. This leads us to the second goal, which is having a group of Board members who are effective community advocates.

## Provide Development Tools and Support for the Board

It is the responsibility of the development team to provide the Board members with the tools and support they need to be effective community advocates. This topic is frequently discussed in nonprofit staff leadership circles. Organizations spend time trying to find the right communication tools or techniques to help educate the important group around the development process. Providing Board members with education and guidance around development is essential. One way to clearly define the role of the Board in development and providing them with the foundation to be effective community advocates is to involve them in the Strategic Development Planning process especially during the stage of creating the compelling case for support and designing impact statements.

A Board member might be at the top of his or her game professionally or socially rich in connections and community involvement. However, none of these are indicators that the individuals on the Board have the background or perspective around what Development is, how it works, or what it means from a Board member perspective. Many will interpret the call for the Board to be involved in Development as, "They want me to ask my friends for money!" This is a common misperception and a real problem. Often it will stop any conversation from happening between the development team and the Board due to the fact that the perspective is they will be asked to do something they are not comfortable with. The organizational leadership should reinforce the strong message that the primary role for a Board member in Development, and the key to them helping grow the donor pool, is to be an effective community advocate. An effective community advocate will:

- Share the case for support with centers of influence and affluence in the community.
- Communicate relevant impact statements and goals based on the audience.
- Identify interest in potential donors—individuals, foundations, and corporations.
- Facilitate introductions to bring together the right member of the organizational staff team and the potential donor.

In order to grow the donor pool, there must be a growing number of individuals aware of the work the nonprofit organization is doing and impact it is having on them or in their community. Effective community advocates are essentially creating connections in the community within the circles of influence and affluence.

Asking for the gift or commitment may be natural for certain Board members. And, it may be appropriate for a particular Board member to make the *ask* or formal solicitation. However, it is not on the list of tasks for an effective community advocate and there should be discussions and agreements around who will be asking for gifts between the leadership team, Board members, and the development executive prior to any active solicitation being made. An *ask*, or formal solicitation is often times more effective when the prospect is presented with the resources and information a team approach offers. The Board member may have the relationship, the Executive Director or President may be the best person to articulate the vision, and a Development Officer may be the most effective at discussing the details of the gift and making sure the gift agreement meets the donor's needs and the mission goals for the organization.

It is the responsibility of the Executive Director, the development executive, and the Board chair to identify each individual Board member's comfort level and optimally his or her role in the development process. It is not a one-step process; it is sequential, organized, and planned. There are four basic stages and they are related and ongoing. Board members can have a role in any or all of those elements or stages. Here is a list of the basic stages of development and some simple examples of how a Board member could participate in that stage:

1. *Identification*—Identify an individual, foundation, or corporation that has a natural connection to the mission of the organization and could provide resources, monetary, in-kind contributions, or collaborative partnership potential to support the efforts to advance the mission of the organization.
2. *Cultivation*—Invite that individual, foundation, or corporate contact to participate in or attend an event or program to personally witness the work of the organization. Facilitate introductions to the appropriate staff at the organization through an event introduction or formal meeting.
3. *Solicitation*—Formally ask for support. If appropriate and agreed upon, as suggested above, make the formal solicitation.
4. *Stewardship*—Show gratitude to supporters. Send personal thank you notes, make phone calls to thank supporters, seek out supporters at events and community activities, and recognize the difference they are making through their support for the organization.

Clearly the members of an organization's Board have an important role in building awareness around the work the organization is doing. They are key communicators in terms of what the organization is doing and how the work of the organization is impacting the community members. The connections each of the Board members has, personally and professionally, and the manner in which they connect the dots between those connections and the organization can provide a very positive direct effect on the growth of the donor pool.

## End of Chapter Review Questions

Here are some questions you should consider and answer after reading this chapter:

- Does your organization's communications strategy address the myriad charitable gift tools the modern donor may use to make contributions to your organization?
- Do you proactively communicate with donors about their gift planning and inquire about their contributions to or involvement in a donor advised fund or private foundation?
- Given the characteristics of the modern donor, does your organization have a communication and development strategy that will attract them and retain their support?
- What is innovative about your communication strategy?
- What is your method for reporting impact and results to donors?
- Have you asked your donors if they are getting the information they want and need to continue their support?
- Are you aware of how your donor pool is evolving?
- What are the conditions affecting your pool?
- Are you proactively adjusting your communication and methods for engaging and cultivating your donors to match the evolving nature of your pool?
- What methods are you employing to grow your donor pool?
- Are you leveraging loyal donor relationships?
- How are you connecting with volunteer and Board member peer groups?
- What is your process for engaging in development cultivation dialogue with volunteers and Board members?
- What is your method and process for engaging Board members in the development process?
- Would you describe your Board members as effective community advocates? If not, why? What can you do to support them in becoming more active and effective?

## Summary

Donors and donor pools are evolving and it is essential that an organization maintain awareness around the changing demographics and expectations of its donor pool. It must anticipate modern donor reporting expectations, be ready to relate dollars invested to impact and results and create new ways to engage with them holistically to understand their gift-planning strategies and not lose its place as a priority in those plans. In addition to the challenges and opportunities around finding ways to retain and deepen existing donor pools is the exercise and responsibility around growing those pools. Fundraising has evolved and the challenges associated with fundraising in this post-Great Recessionary environment, with more than one million nonprofits competing for the same limited dollars, must be addressed through a collaborative effort and commitment between the Board and staff. The development team alone cannot realize the success that group commitment will bring to the fund-raising efforts.

Next up is a look at some of the evolving expectations around charity efficiency. The modern donor is not just focused on results and impact, they have newfound expectations around transparency of nonprofit policies and practices. They are holding organizations and Boards accountable for high standards and practices.

# CHAPTER 14

# Growing Expectations
*Nonprofit Efficiency—Ratings, Ratios, Information, and Insight*

To prosper, and frankly to survive in this competitive environment, nonprofit efficiency is essential. The environment has changed; there is a whole new lens the modern donor is looking through when making decisions about where to allocate their philanthropic dollars. The donors are holding the nonprofit accountable and they expect transparency. It's no longer a question of *if* the organization wants to disclose information; it's just a matter of where to find it. Donors want to know that the organization has adopted policies and prudent practices across the board, including prudent investment management, cost control for spending, compliance around IRS standards, and integrity and credibility around fund development. They have myriad tools at their fingertips to conduct the research necessary to determine the nonprofit's efficiency and this trend is changing how Boards conduct their business and how staff operates the nonprofit. Nonprofit efficiency and transparency matter to nonprofits because they matter to those who donate.

More significantly, as was discussed in the chapters covering development and fundraising trends and truths, this evolving group of donors are in control of the estimated $41 trillion which will be generationally transferred over the next 25 years and this group of modern donors—the baby boomers, gen X and Y alike—are demanding nonprofits be accountable and transparent around their policies and practices. These groups have witnessed many scandals in the nonprofit and financial sectors. They have learned to be critical and require proof of results and effectiveness. The days when any nonprofit could remain unresponsive to donors, lack transparency, and continue to receive support are long gone. Donors are now conditioned through the rating agencies and the media to focus on evaluating nonprofits' organizational efficiency and organizational capacity.

# Resources

There has been an evolution in the number of resources available to compare and rate nonprofits and guide donors through the process of evaluating and comparing nonprofits. These resources provide impartial examination of organizational financial health and efficiencies; many include ratings or scores. Some donors, more than others, rely on these scores since they come from an impartial examination. Studies have shown that high net worth households in their 60s depend less frequently on rating agencies than a younger generation donor might. In any case, the modern donor will use all of the tools available to them in order to ensure they are investing in an organization that is being run efficiently and is effectively reaching its mission goals.

## The IRS Form 990

To maintain its tax exempt status, a nonprofit organization is required to submit a tax return, called the Form 990, to the Internal Revenue Service. This form was recently updated to provide even more information than the original version. It now includes information addressing best practices around governance and nonprofit policies, in addition to expanded detail regarding revenue and expenses. The Board and executive leadership should become familiar with the newly revised Form 990, which was modified with the idea that forcing nonprofits to disclose more information would prevent fraud and abuse.

As of 2010, every organization with assets of $500,000 and gross receipts over $200,000 must use the new Form 990. Before Form 990 was revised, some nonprofits simply deposited the form on the desk of the chief financial officer to take care of in the normal course of business. Given the complexity of the issues to be discussed and then described in Form 990, it is more essential than ever that the executive director, chief financial officer, legal counsel, and CPA review the 990 before it is submitted. Additionally, the new form also reinforces the Board's fiduciary responsibility by requiring formal acknowledgement of Board review of the completed form prior to it being filed with the IRS.

Donors today are more likely than in previous generations to question how the nonprofit is being run, in part because information about charities is more readily accessible than ever before. It is easy for them to check the nonprofit's IRS Form 990 tax return, using www.guidestar.org or www .foundationcenter.org, to see, among other things, what the operating expense ratio is, how much the highest executives at a nonprofit are getting paid, where the revenue is coming from, and if all of the standard policies are in place. Because of its tax status, and the realities of its situation, most nonprofits are in effect an open book.

## Governance, Disclosure, and the New Form 990

In 2008 the IRS introduced the new 990 in response to the tremendous rise in the number of nonprofits and increasing occurrences of nonprofit sector scandals. Highly compensated nonprofit executives and countless examples of conflicts of interest brought dysfunctional nonprofit organization issues to the forefront in the press and most importantly a heightened awareness to donors. In addition to rollout of the new 990, a new sense of entitlement around information accessibility by major donors and philanthropists was born. Prior to this rise in awareness and understanding around policy and practices, donors counted on simple calculations showing sound fiscal fitness. If an organization had low operational costs it was good as gold.

The IRS redesigned the Form 990, incorporating elements encouraging nonprofit leadership to implement sound governance practices and prudent fiduciary oversight. The changes to nonprofit governance and reporting requirements are meant to prevent individuals from gaining improper financial advantage through charitable work, improve oversight of fiscal conduct, and to create greater organizational transparency for donors, potential donors, and the public in general.

The newly designed form requires myriad details including information on fundraising expenses, fundraising registration, public contributions, non-cash contributions, loans, lobbying activities, and expenses. In addition, the new Form 990 includes multiple questions regarding governance and requires the organization to disclose whether or not it has adopted a number of policies and practices including:

- If the organization has independent directors and if so, how many
- Conflict of interest policy—*Does the organization have the policy and is it consistently reviewed, monitored, and enforced?*
- Whistleblower policy—*Does the organization have the policy and does it contain all of the elements to protect an employee from retaliation if he or she brings an inappropriate activity to the Board?*
- Document retention and destruction policy—*Does the organization have the policy and does it outline the length of time records will be kept, where they will be kept, and how they will be disposed of?*
- Meeting documentation—*Are all Board meetings and decisions documented?*

There are several more changes not listed here.

## Special Attention to Fundraising Disclosures and Executive Compensation

There are various sections of the form that are too intricate to fully describe here, but there are detailed questions and information that must be provided, addressing both fundraising disclosures and executive compensation that Board members and executive leadership should be familiar with, such as:

## Fundraising Disclosures

- The types of fundraising activities used by the organization
- Existence of fundraising agreements with individuals (including directors, officers, trustees, or key employees) or entities for fundraising services, and a list of the 10 highest-paid fundraisers including, for each, an accounting of gross amounts raised and amount paid to or retained by the nonprofit
- List of all states where the organization is registered or licensed to solicit funds
- For each fundraising event (including gaming), a listing of gross receipts, charitable contributions, cash prizes, non-cash prizes, rent/facility costs, and other direct expenses

## Compensation Disclosures

- The names and compensation details for the top five highest-paid employees and independent contractors of $100,000 or more.
- For individuals receiving more than $150,000 in compensation, the compensation detail is to be broken out between the base compensation, bonus and incentive compensation, other compensation deferred compensation, and non-taxable compensation.
- Additional compensation questions must be responded to for high-income earners over $150,000, such as:
  - Did the organization pay for first-class or charter travel?
  - Did the organization pay for travel for companions?
  - Did the organization provide a discretionary spending account?
  - Did the organization provide a housing allowance?
  - Did the organization make payments for the business use of a personal residence?
  - Did the organization make payments for health or social club dues/fees?
  - Did the organization provide personal services; that is, a chef, maid, chauffeur, or the like?

Between the press and the Form 990's focus in this area, there has been a tremendous amount of awareness around nonprofit executive compensation. Relatively speaking, nonprofit executives are compensated at below for-profit standards and they generally do not work in lavish offices. The *Chronicle of Philanthropy* (www.philanthropy.com) annually displays the compensation of the nation's top paid nonprofit executives. These days, in the recovery after the Great Recession, most charities have focused great attention on balancing the need to fairly compensate competent professional staff to retain them while recognizing the need to allocate scarce financial resources to meet their charitable missions. That said, there have been numerous issues around the public's perception of fair compensation for nonprofit executives and a heightened awareness by the IRS around this line item on the Form 990. An organization's Board should have an Executive Compensation policy outlining the thought process and philosophy around making executive compensation decisions. Having the policy in place will facilitate answering the questions on the 990 and prepare them for any additional questions that may come about from the IRS or donors around the compensation decisions.

## Two Key Measures of Financial Health

There are two general areas of financial health that are most closely scrutinized by rating agencies, and all foundations and endowments are scored in both areas. These are *organizational efficiency* and *organizational capacity.*

Charity Navigator (www.charitynavigator.org), a widely respected nonprofit rating organization, is an independent, nonprofit organization that evaluates nonprofits with a stated goal of advancing a more efficient and responsive philanthropic marketplace by evaluating the financial health of America's largest charities. Charity Navigator has developed a system for scoring financial health as well as accountability and transparency of nonprofits. Many in the industry, as well as potential donors, have come to rely on its evaluation and rating system. Charity Navigator, along with other rating organizations like GuideStar, The American Institute of Philanthropy, and The Better Business Bureau, employ certain financial ratios or performance categories to rate nonprofits. In so doing, they depend on the financial information each nonprofit lists on its tax returns or on the Form 990.

In addition to establishing a score in each of the areas of organizational efficiency and capacity, they can also give an overall rating that depicts the nonprofit's efficiency performance by combining the two scores. This is a form of shorthand that can be very helpful to a potential donor.

### Organizational Efficiency

Simply stated, efficient charities spend less to raise more money. Another way of putting it is that efficient charities spend less on administrative costs and a higher percentage on the programs and services they support. In general, there are four performance areas that donors and rating agencies scrutinize in determining the efficiency of a nonprofit: fundraising efficiency, program expenses, administrative expenses, and organizational capacity. A rating is established in each of these areas and from them comes a combined rating to reflect a positive or negative ratio of expenses to distribution.

These ratios are typically converted into a rating score, a number, or a symbol. These two scores are intended to reflect a nonprofit's efficiency in a specific category and to allow comparison with its peers.

Reports of poor nonprofit efficiency appear routinely in the national media. In the coming years, nonprofit efficiency will become increasingly significant to the success and survival of every American nonprofit. Consider it this way: The worth of any nonprofit is determined by the success of meeting its charitable mission and by the low cost of its own fundraising and administration. This is, in part, because the key question for most potential modern donors is whether or not the money they are considering giving will be put to a good and worthy use.

**FUNDRAISING EXPENSES**   A nonprofit development team and staff leadership should be reviewing the cost effectiveness of its fundraising strategy regularly. Reviewing financial resource allocation and return on investment for fundraising strategies should be conducted during the creation of the Strategic Development Plan. Many nonprofits continue to invest heavily in direct mail campaigns.

Here are some sample questions related to evaluating a direct mail campaign that the development team and executive leadership should be addressing around fundraising cost efficiency:

- Is the direct mail campaign an effective use of fundraising resources?
- What was the response rate?
- How many new donors did we engage with this mailing?
- What is the cost of the campaign compared to the revenue received (ROI)?
- Is it our most effective technique for fundraising?
- What else does the mailing offer us apart from direct revenue? Is there a mission- or marketing-related element tied to communicating our impact?
- Are the expenses appropriately allocated to reflect the benefits we receive from the direct mail campaign?

Although many nonprofits continue to invest heavily in direct mail campaigns, they may just be doing what they have always done. In some cases, especially for those nonprofits of long standing with well-established income streams, it can be easy to slip into complacency and allow overhead and fundraising costs to grow disproportionately. A traditional, very successful nonprofit can become a victim of its own success and reputation. That is why it is important for an organization to evaluate whether the financial resources being applied to a direct mail campaign, for example, could be better applied using other strategies. Direct mail is just one example of a fundraising technique; it is important to evaluate all of the fundraising activities in this same way.

To be an effective nonprofit, and to attract the sophisticated modern donor, an organization must have an efficient fundraising strategy. The amount spent to raise money must be an acceptable, even a desirable, percentage of what is ultimately collected. Fundraising efficiency is simply how much a nonprofit spends for each dollar collected. This is determined by dividing fundraising expenses by the total of contributions it receives as a consequence. For example, if $100,000 is spent to raise $200,000, the fundraising efficiency is $0.50. But if the nonprofit spends the same $100,000 and raises $1 million, than its fundraising efficiency is $0.10. It is best practice for an organization to spend no more than 25 percent of its budget on fundraising and administrative fees.

The costs of fundraising tend to increase over time. There are the increasing cost associated with the operations and administration of running a nonprofit, the technology and sophisticated marketing strategies needed to reach the multi-generational group of prospects, the cost of adding or replacing qualified and experienced fundraising staff, and finally the inherent cost to acquiring new donors to grow the evolving donor pool. Keeping all of these costs in line can be a challenge. However, organizational leadership must manage these factors directly affecting the fundraising efficiency in order to stay ahead of the game amongst the growing competition.

**PROGRAM EXPENSES**　Nonprofits exist to support worthy causes that promote the social good. Accordingly, most of every nonprofit's annual budget should be allocated toward its programs and services. It is best practice for a nonprofit to spend at least 75 percent of its total expenses on program activities. When analysts are calculating this ratio to compare program expenses of one nonprofit to another, they divide program expenses by a nonprofit's total expenses. For example, if a nonprofit spends $5 million on its program expenses with a total operating budget of $6 million, it spends 83 percent on program expenses, an excellent state of affairs. However, it is important to be cautious about giving too much weight to this number. An examination of the ratios across the nonprofit sector will show that there is a range of percentages spent on programs and it may vary by type of nonprofit. Therefore, this ratio comparison is not always an accurate gauge of one organization being more efficient than another.

Additionally, organizational leadership should be tying the program expenses to the program effectiveness. What this means is if a nonprofit's mission is to make a profound impact on a select group of individuals, they may need to spend a bigger percentage on programs and services to meet their mission goals. This is a critical area for Board and executive leadership discussion. It may not always be prudent to take the least expensive route in terms of budgeting around programing

**ADMINISTRATIVE EXPENSES**   The ratio of administrative expenses to other costs is a matter of concern to all potential donors. A nonprofit must have a place of business, talented staff, and skilled administrators to do well, but the costs for these must not be allowed to become disproportionate. To calculate this ratio, take the administrative costs of a nonprofit and divide them by the nonprofit's total expenses. For example, if a nonprofit spends $400,000 in administrative costs out of total expenses of $4.7 million, it is expending 8.5 percent on administrative expenses, again, a very good ratio.

These ratios, and their average, determine the organizational efficiency and allow comparison of one nonprofit to another. As scores are adjusted into the disadvantageous range, donors may begin to notice, and such adverse ratings will have a damaging effect on the nonprofit and its mission. That is why it is critical for the leadership team to communicate the reasoning in the most transparent way to loyal donors and passionate prospects, especially if the numbers are not favorable to the nonprofit's peer group in the sector. Sometimes it is necessary and beneficial for the organization to spend more on resources to receive more benefits.

A recent study conducted by the Nonprofit Research Collaborative showed a direct link between the investment an organization made in its fundraising resources and the fundraising results. Additionally, the study also showed a direct correlation between a nonprofit failing to invest in fundraising and failing to meet its goals.[1] Many nonprofits are discovering that it is sometimes necessary to spend money in order to make more money. However, the decision to add staff and increase administrative expenses must be thoughtful and by no means should the decision cause a strain the budget. In any case, if the decision is made to increase administrative or fundraising expenses significantly, leadership must design transparent communication around strategic objectives to support potentially short-term increased expenses for long-term increased revenue.

---

[1] "The 2010 Nonprofit Fundraising Survey," Nonprofit Research Collaborative, March 2011, http://foundationcenter.org/gainknowledge/research/pdf/nrc_survey2011.pdf.

## Organizational Capacity

How does a donor know that a nonprofit will be able to sustain itself and its programs during and beyond times of economic upheaval? An organization's ability to support its services and programs over a period of time even in the face of adversity is what is meant by organizational capacity. Building organizational capacity should be an integral part of the normal operation and evolution of a nonprofit. We know that through the 2008 and 2009 recession, large charities, including Ivy League schools, had their organizational capacities tested and have had to curtail building programs, delay other infrastructure projects, and suspend certain operational outlays. It is desirable that a nonprofit plan for the long term and not allow its resources to become so diminished that it must devote time and effort to short-term fundraising to meet predictable financial demands.

Like all living organisms, charities must grow to survive and serve the needs of those to whom they give. Primarily, growth for a nonprofit means an ever-increasing stream of donations from a wide range of sources. This can include contributions by individuals and bequests, as well as donations from corporations, foundations, and the government. It also includes membership dues and program revenue of various types, as well as fees and contracts. A nonprofit should, at the minimum, expect to consistently outpace inflation in revenue growth. If it doesn't, it will find itself in very serious trouble.

As there is an increase in revenue growth, a nonprofit should have balanced growth in the programs and services it supports. If a nonprofit is narrowly focused on one mission, it is reasonable to expect the efforts it supports for that mission to constantly expand. If a nonprofit has a broader focus then it will routinely be addressing the needs of a greater constituency. In either case, the well-balanced nonprofit will continue to support the increasing needs of society by staying focused on its mission-based goals. Further, if a nonprofit takes the steps to gain greater efficiency and is *seen* by the public as being efficient, donors will be more inclined to support the nonprofit and its mission.

Adequate working capital is important to all charities as they rely on their reserves to survive difficult times. These can include a poorly performing economy or disasters which tend to draw a great volume of donations from their usual donor pool. Lacking an adequate reserve often means letting valuable staff go, dropping important programs, acquiring debt, merging with another nonprofit, or even dissolving altogether.

But those charities with an adequate reserve do not face such difficult decisions. In fact, by working at building organizational capacity annually, in part through an increase in working capital, an organization will have a greater ability to enhance existing programs and add new ones.

How long a nonprofit can sustain its current programs absent new revenue is a factor of its capital reserve. A ratio can be used to rate a nonprofit and allow its comparison in this area with other charities. One method used to evaluate a nonprofit's working capital ratio is to divide its working capital by total expenses, including its distributions to existing services and programs, for the last fiscal year. For example, if a nonprofit has $4.5 million in reserve and its total expenses for the most recent fiscal year were $2.8 million, it has a working capital ratio of 1.6 years. This ratio is then compared to peer charities as a measure of organizational capacity.

## Overall Scores and Ratings

Once ratings are established in the categories that encompass organizational efficiency and capacity, the ratings can be combined and converted into a raw score using a number scale and or star rating representing a nonprofit's score for organizational efficiency and a separate one for organizational capacity.

Finally, a grand score that represents a nonprofit's *state of affairs* is calculated, and the nonprofit is given an overall rating and/or a star score depending on the rating agency. Most donors who take the time to learn a certain nonprofit's rating never go beyond these two scores.

**NOT ALL SCORES ARE CREATED EQUAL**   While some charities are quite similar, it is not possible to force all of them into the same mold. Every nonprofit to one degree or another has its own unique DNA. Identical management practices and charitable impulses can produce very different scores for certain charities. As mentioned earlier, some charitable causes lend themselves to a certain type of fundraising that can affect fundraising costs positively or negatively. Some charities of necessity must have a presence in certain high-rent districts, while others can successfully operate from an obscure office on a back street.

Food banks, for example typically deploy and distribute the money and in-kind donations (food) they receive rather than using it to build an endowment. This would be a standard practice for them given the nature of what they do. It is actually in their best interest to spend/give away almost everything that they receive in a given year versus setting it aside for future years in order to meet their mission goals. This means the organization can be successful, and well managed, with very little capital reserve.

A community foundation in the same city would likely be a very different matter. Such foundations typically hold reserves that can sustain them for several years. These two types of charities must be considered in a different light because their raw scores could present a false picture of the reality. Adjustments are required in their scores so they can be properly rated.

Charities should not be ranked. It simply isn't a practical option and can be very misleading. Charities can be compared, one to another, or within a peer group, but time should be taken to examine scores in various categories and to understand what went into establishing the rating.

Of note, recently Charity Navigator's rating system has evolved and expanded to include not only an evaluation of an organization's financial health, but it is also examining accountability and transparency factors, which they define as follows:

- *Accountability* is an obligation or willingness by a nonprofit to explain its actions to its stakeholders. For now, Charity Navigator is specifically evaluating the fiduciary actions of charities. In the future, we intend to evaluate other aspects of accountability such as results reporting and other indicators of the way nonprofits use the resources they raise to accomplish their mission.
- *Transparency* is an obligation or willingness by a nonprofit to publish and make available critical data about the organization.

This system is much more comprehensive than the standard system based on fiscal efficiencies and it includes an evaluation of an organization's Form 990 and a review of the information available on its website.

Not everyone depends on Charity Navigator for information and analysis. However, it is important for board members and nonprofit leadership and staff to be familiar with the rating agency trends and Charity Navigator certainly seems to be positing itself as a trendsetter when it comes to providing valuable quality ratings around nonprofit accountability and transparency standards. In that same vein, every board member and non-profit executive should be familiar with each organization's rating and the measurement standards of each of the sites and systems and they should know their organization's scores. It is advisable for the nonprofit leadership team to also be familiar with The Better Business Bureau (BBB) Wise Giving Alliance Standards for Charitable Accountability, which can be accessed through www.bbb.org/us/charity. The standards include specific details in the areas of governance and oversight, measuring effectiveness, finances and fund raising, and informational materials.

## Financial Ratios

There is a great deal of discussion and debate around the value and weight given to a nonprofit's financial ratios. It is important to have perspective around the importance of each rating and every area of potential measurement for nonprofit efficiency and effectiveness. The numbers will most often not always tell the full story about the impact and effectiveness of the organization and they certainly won't reflect the organization's changing needs based on where they are in their lifecycles. Organizational leadership must understand the ratios and ratings, but they must also be prepared to support the decisions they have made and articulate the case for those decisions to prospects and donors. It is essential to keep this in mind in this chapter.

In rating nonprofits, the ratios used include:

- *Operating Ratio.* The most commonly used ratio, also known as the Current Ratio. It reflects how well a nonprofit can meet its short-term debt obligations; that is, short-term liquidity. The ratio is determined by dividing total assets by total liabilities. An Operating Ratio of one or greater is considered desirable.
- *Debt/Equity Ratio.* This is the most commonly used measure of long-term liquidity. Long-term debt is divided by total net assets to arrive at the ratio. A better measure excludes assets that are permanently restricted for one reason or another.
- *Financial Flexibility Ratios.* The flexibility here is the structure of the portfolio and how it is managed. Fixed assets, such as buildings, are considered to be less flexible than stocks, as an example. The ratio is calculated by taking fixed assets and dividing them by total assets. A score close to one indicates less flexibility.
- *Net Income Ratio.* Nonprofits ideally zero out at the end of the fiscal year. If they have significant sums on hand which are not immediately redirected to programs, then it reflects poorly on management and the nonprofit's commitment to its programs.

These ratios are a useful supplement to the others. Ratio analysis is its own specialized field and, properly conducted, can provide very valuable information when comparing one nonprofit to another.

Nonprofits must share data with potential donors to appear sufficiently transparent. An organization's image is vital and most managers understand that, but potential donors must not struggle to understand a nonprofit's finances. A nonprofit must not only conduct itself with propriety and financial efficiency, it must be seen as doing so.

In referring to the study of high net worth households,[2] more than 50 percent of the donors surveyed indicated that a nonprofit's demonstration of

---

[2] The 2010 Study of High Net Worth Philanthropy sponsored by Bank of America Merrill Lynch.

sound business practices and appropriate overhead spending in the top five of their top priority factors when making a charitable gift.

## Integrity and Credibility

In this era when donors have the daunting task of determining which charities deserve their hard-earned donations, they are met with an over-abundance of choices. Currently, there are more than one million public charities in the United States. If there are an estimated 314 million Americans, then by implication, there is a nonprofit for every 314 people. With the shocking number of charities all looking for funds from a limited number of affluent individuals, it is striking to us that many charities don't recognize the importance of insuring that best practices are adhered to, just to compete in the nonprofit marketplace.

Experts have suggested that in order for nonprofits to grow their public support, nonprofits must:

- *Be Transparent*. Donors and those seeking to donate must be able to readily learn about the nonprofit to which they want to give. An open and informative (less common than you might think) website is a very efficient means for accomplishing this.
- *Show Results*. Today's donors want to know they are making a difference. They are willing to give large sums to specific charities, but only if they can see that the nonprofit is actually doing something positive with their money.
- *Do What They Do Best*. Doing what you do best means making an assessment of current programs and winding down or jettisoning programs that other charities do better.
- *Stay in Touch with Donors, but Don't Harass Them*. Surveys continue to show that donors do not want to be over solicited.

In addition to the suggestions listed above, nonprofits should follow best fundraising practices and:

- Adopt the Association of Fundraising Professionals Code of Ethical Principles and Standards and Donor Bill of Rights.
- Post the documents on its website and make them readily available to donors.
- Create a fundraising policy and procedure document.

Because of adverse sensationalized publicity and poor reporting practices, charities are under ever-growing scrutiny, and there is a movement afoot to impose even greater controls and regulations upon them.

## End of Chapter Review Questions

Here are some questions you should consider and answer after reading this chapter:

- Do you know what your nonprofit is rated with each of the rating agencies?
- Are you familiar with all of the criteria under which rating agencies are measuring and comparing nonprofits?
- Are you familiar with your nonprofit's ratios? How does your organization compare to similar type nonprofits in the sector?
- If your ratios are not favorable, do you know why?
- Are you comfortable with all of the answers to the questions on the IRS Form 990?
- Have you reviewed your Form 990? Do you understand it as well as your donors may?

## Summary

Donors are becoming more resourceful and the information and analysis being made available to them is abundant. The reality of heightened visibility around nonprofit organizational capacity and efficiency is not going to reverse itself. Individuals are becoming more familiar with the information contained in the new Form 990 and developing clarity around the meaning of each component. Rating agencies are becoming more focused on accountability and transparency as they move further away from depending on financial ratios and turn toward analyzing holistic factors reflecting organizational capacity and efficiency. And it is almost certain that the IRS will become increasingly more tuned in to the information contained in the Form 990.

The key for nonprofits to thrive in this fishbowl environment is first and foremost for the Board and staff to have a clear understanding of the organization's numbers, ratings, and ratios alike. Secondly, and equally critical, is for the organization's representatives, volunteers, and staff to be able to clearly articulate the story behind the numbers. This means they should understand and be able to communicate strategy and vision around growth, which may be temporarily increasing expenses. Or, it could mean standing behind what may be perceived as a risky decision or practice that, in reality, was a thoughtful decision made by prudent fiduciaries.

Like any good relationship, clear, honest communication is the key to success with donors in this environment of growing expectations.

# Conclusion

In closing, we recognize that every nonprofit is unique—in its mission, its leadership, its fundraising, and its portfolio. However, we believe the keys to success in this new reality are the same for all organizations: prudent practices, consistent processes, and sound policies around investment and development strategies alike.

It is our hope that no matter what role you hold in your organization, volunteer or staff, the insight you gathered from this book will provide you with the tools and techniques to help your organization grow. Our intention is to provide you with resources and information that will continue to be relevant no matter what the state of our economy.

Key points to keep in mind as you do your work include:

- Have a clear vision for the future
- Be prepared for change
- Protect the mission
- Continuously update and maintain sound policies and governance practices
- Collaborate and partner with trusted advisors familiar with the sector
- Avoid unnecessary risks
- Develop meaningful relationships
- Diversify your revenue sources
- Embrace transparency
- Recognize and measure your impact
- Know how to tell your story

# About the Companion Website

The companion website to *Nonprofit Investment and Development* provides readers with sample templates, resources, and essential links to assist them in working through the suggested practices and strategies throughout this book.

Please visit www.wiley.com/go/nonprofitsolutions to find the following links and materials, categorized by chapter.

## Chapter 2 Fiduciary Responsibility

- Sample Templates
  - Sample outline for new board member education
- Essential Links
  - UPMIFA, http://uniformlaws.org
  - IRS Resources for nonprofits, www.irs.gov/Charities-&-Non-Profits
  - Investment Management Consultants Association, www.imca.org
  - Charity Navigator, www.charitynavigator.org
  - GuideStar, www.guidestar.org
  - BoardSource, www.boardsource.org

## Chapter 3 New Roles for the "New Reality"

- Sample Templates
  - Evaluation checklist of advisor services
  - Question guide for selecting an investment advisor
- Essential Links
  - Nonprofit Assistance Fund, www.nonprofitsassistancefund.org/index .php?src=gendocs&ref=FMN_Investment_and_Endowment_Policies& category=Healthy%20Financial%20Practices

## Chapter 5 Understanding Risk

- Sample Templates
  - Allocation and Risk Questionnaire

## Chapter 6 Asset Allocation

- Sample Templates
  - Allocation and Risk Questionnaire

## Chapter 7 Investment Policy Statement (IPS)

- Sample Templates
  - Sample Investment Audit Questionnaire
  - Sample Investment Policy Statement
  - Sample Spending Policy

## Chapter 11 Socially Responsible Investing

- Sample Templates
  - Questionnaire for assessing socially responsible investing criteria

## Chapter 13 The Evolution of Donors—Trends and Truths

- Sample Templates
  - Volunteer leadership/board member questionnaire
  - Volunteer leadership menu of engagement

## Chapter 14 Growing Expectations

- Essential Links
  - IRS Governance Check Sheet, www.irs.gov/pub/irs-tege/governance_check_sheet.pdf
  - BoardSource, www.boardsource.org/Knowledge.asp
  - IRS Good Governance Practices, www.irs.gov/pub/irs-tege/governance_practices.pdf

# About the Authors

## Roger M. Matloff

Roger has over 30 years of experience as an investment professional. He currently works for a world leading investment bank as the founder of an institutional consulting team specializing in serving the nonprofit market. In this role, Roger oversees analytical investment management programs for an extensive number of the team's foundation and endowment clients, as well as providing philanthropic consulting on an institutional level. He also oversees the development of customized asset allocation models, due diligence of investment managers through the application of qualitative and quantitative analysis, and the continuous monitoring of performance to ensure clients' investment objectives are met.

Roger graduated with honors from Rutgers University with a degree in Economics and received an MBA in Finance and Deterministic Optimization Modeling. Roger completed studies of Market Theory and Econometrics at Oxford University under a private foundation grant. He was subsequently chosen by the same foundation to study Political Economic Theory at Dartmouth College. He is a Certified Investment Management Analyst, Accredited Investment Fiduciary, and Accredited Retirement Plan Consultant, as well as a Chartered Advisor in Philanthropy.

Roger has appeared on ABC, CBS, and Fox affiliates. He has been cited in the *Wall Street Journal* and Wall Street's industry publication, *Research*. Roger co-authored the books, *Molecular Investment Consulting for Philanthropies: A Holistic Approach for Nonprofit Management* and *Thriving in the Comets Tail: Nonprofit Investment and Development during the Recovery from the Great Recession.*

## Joy Hunter Chaillou

Joy has over 18 years of experience in the nonprofit and investment management industries, including six years at the American Heart Association serving as a Vice President of Planned Giving and National Planned Giving Marketing Committee Chair. She currently serves as a consultant working with nonprofit organizations of all sizes to increase their organizational capacity and thrive by offering in-depth strategies and tailored solutions, providing them with the knowledge and resources needed to address the challenges they face as they pursue their missions and impact goals. Joy's advice and consultation focus in the areas of governance, development strategies, staff training, and board education.

Joy is an active and engaged board member for Girl's Inc. Westchester and the Children's Support Foundation. She is a founding board member for the Association of Fundraising Professionals chapter in Westchester, New York, where she currently serves as the Vice President of Membership. She is proud to serve as the co-Chair for the American Heart Association's Heart Advisory Committee on Long Island and serves on the Professional Advisory Committees for the Central Park Conservancy, Lighthouse International, and the New Jersey Symphony Orchestra.

Joy earned her B.S. from Old Dominion University through the Centre d'Etude Franco-Américain de Management (CEFAM) and her M.B.A. from Dominican University of California.

# Index